UNDERSTANDING SABERMETRICS

An Introduction to the Science of Baseball Statistics

Gabriel B. Costa,
Michael R. Huber *and*
John T. Saccoman

McFarland & Company, Inc., Publishers
Jefferson, North Carolina, and London

LIBRARY OF CONGRESS CATALOGUING-IN-PUBLICATION DATA

Costa, Gabriel B.
   Understanding sabermetrics : an introduction to the science
of baseball statistics / Gabriel B. Costa, Michael R. Huber and
John T. Saccoman.
      p.   cm.
   Includes bibliographical references and index.

   ISBN-13: 978-0-7864-3388-9
   softcover : 50# alkaline paper ∞

   1. Baseball.   2. Baseball—Statistics.   3. Baseball—Miscellanea.
I. Huber, Michael R., 1960–   II. Saccoman, John T., 1964–
III. Title.
GV867.C67   2008
796.357—dc22

                                          2007042474

British Library cataloguing data are available

Cover image ©2008 Shutterstock

Manufactured in the United States of America

McFarland & Company, Inc., Publishers
   Box 611, Jefferson, North Carolina 28640
   www.mcfarlandpub.com

Table of Contents

Acknowledgments

MY NAME IS GABE COSTA. I am a Catholic priest and a mathematician, and I have been crazy about baseball since 1958, when I first learned about the game at the age of ten. At the time of this writing, I am on an extended academic leave from the Department of Mathematics and Computer Science at Seton Hall University, presently teaching mathematics at the United States Military Academy, West Point, New York, where I also assist the post chaplains. Toward the end of these acknowledgments, you will hear from my coauthors, Mike Huber of Muhlenberg College and John T. Saccoman of Seton Hall University.

In a sense, this book came about because of my oldest friend, Frank Mottola. We met in 1953 in the kindergarten at Sadie F. Leinkauf School in Hoboken, New Jersey. Frank and I have been friends ever since. In the early 1980s, Frank mentioned something about a book titled *The Bill James Baseball Abstract*; in fact, he gave me several annual editions. It was James who introduced the term "sabermetrics" (derived from SABR, the acronym for the Society for American Baseball Research), defining it as the search for objective knowledge about baseball. After I devoured these books, I approached the academic and administrative leaders at Seton Hall University with a proposal to teach a new one-credit course: MATH 1011: Sabermetrics.

Through the efforts of Dr. Dan Gross, Dr. Jane Norton and Dr. John J. Saccoman (the father of one of the coauthors of this book), Seton Hall approved the course for the 1988 winter session. I believe that this was one of the first (if not *the* first) Sabermetrics courses ever offered for college or university credit. And the course is still running. We are indebted to these three educators for their support. In 1996, United States Army Lieutenant Colonel William Fox (now retired), his associate Major Mike Huber (now a retired lieutenant colonel) and I introduced a three-credit course at West Point on sabermetrics — MA 488, which is still offered.

While this book is partially an outgrowth of these courses, it is primarily motivated by love and desire: a love for the game of baseball, and a desire to introduce the reader to the rudiments of Sabermetrics. Our goal has been to provide the reader with a sufficient number of quantitative instruments to assist him/her with the measurements of the accomplishments of individual players and various teams, while at the same time providing a qualitative backdrop which would assist objective evaluations. Walking this line was not always easy, but we trust that those who enjoy statistics will be satisfied with our expositions and that our mathematical rigor will also be appreciated by fans who do not necessarily wish to follow every nuance of the mathematical details. With the exception of the first chapter, the last chapter and the appendix, we have pretty much kept the mathematics to basic arithmetic, statistics and a bit of algebra. We assure you that you will not find any references to the fundamental theorem of calculus.

Each of the three of us has his own way of writing. We have tried to unify our approach, but the reader will undoubtedly notice differences in our styles. We trust that this will give the reader different perspectives for looking at the game of baseball. The reader will also find that some chapters are longer than others, due to the nature of the topics. We have titled most of them "innings"; some innings (really *half*-innings) are completed quickly with three pitches, while others take much time. Furthermore, we have purposely left some questions unanswered, leaving the reader to arrive at his/her own conclusions.

Because more and more institutions of higher learning are offering courses related to sabermetrics (e.g., Bowling Green State University, Tufts University and others), we have provided the reader with a number of problems at the end of each chapter, the purpose of which is to illustrate the salient points of the specific topics which have been covered in that chapter. We trust the reader will have fun answering these baseball questions while strengthening his/her ability to reason "sabermetrically."

We also provide what we have termed an "educational module" in an appendix. Because this book can be used as a text for a course in sabermetrics, the module can serve as a primer for the instructor and the student. We three authors have taught courses on sabermetrics, individually or with colleagues, dozens of times, ranging over a period of nearly two decades. This appendix covers such topics as course prerequisites, objectives, content, and assessment tools. It is our hope that this feature will prove helpful and encourage other institutions to offer a course on sabermetrics.

I would like to thank my Archbishop, Most Reverend John J. Myers. In every sense, his guidance and support have been a blessing.

From Seton Hall University, I am grateful to the Priest Community, ministered to by Monsignor James M. Cafone, to my colleagues in the Department of Mathematics and Computer Science, chaired by Dr. Joan Guetti, and to Dean Joseph Marbach and Associate Dean Parviz Ansari of the College of Arts and Sciences. Thank you from the bottom of my heart.

Lastly, to Colonel Michael Phillips and the entire Department of Mathematical Sciences at the United States Military Academy, thank you for your friendship and support.

MICHAEL R. HUBER: In addition to thanking my coauthors, I would like to thank my colleagues at the United States Military Academy who assisted us in our sabermetrics course: Jeff Broadwater, Scott Billie, Alex Heidenberg, Mike Phillips, Andy Glen, and Rod Sturdivant. I want to thank Gabriel Schechter and Jim Gates of the National Baseball Hall of Fame and Museum, for always welcoming our classes and devoting their precious time to teaching our students about sabermetrics.

JOHN T. SACCOMAN: I would like to thank my coauthors, who are equally mathematicians and baseball men, not mere dabblers in either. Baseball and mathematics are our avocations, and it is a rare pleasure to find such kindred spirits.

Pre-Game: Abbreviations and Formulas

Batting

G = Games played

AB = At-bats

H = Hits

BB = Bases on balls (Walks)

IBB = Intentional bases on balls

HP = Hit by pitch

R = Runs scored

RBI = Runs batted in

1B = Singles

2B = Doubles

3B = Triples

HR = Home runs

BA = Batting Average = H / AB

OBA = On-base average = (H + BB + HP) / (AB + BB + HP)

TB = Total bases = 1(1B) + 2(2B) + 3(3B) + 4(HR)

SLG = Slugging average = TB / AB

OPS = On-base plus slugging = OBA + SLG

ISO = Isolated power = SLG − BA = (TB − H) / AB

TPQ = Total power quotient = (HR + RBI + TB) / AB

PwrF = Power factor = SLG/BA = TB/H

SF = Sacrifice flies

SH = Sacrifice hits (Bunts)

Base Running

SB = Stolen bases
CS = Caught stealing
OOB = Outs on base

Pitching

W = Wins
L = Losses
PCT = Winning percentage = W / (W + L)
ER = Earned Runs allowed
IP = Innings pitched
ERA = Earned run average = 9 × ER / IP
SV = Saves
K = Strikeouts
BB = Bases on balls (allowed)

Fielding

A = Assists
E = Errors
PO = Putouts
FLD = Fielding average = (A + PO) / (A + PO + E)
RF = Range factor (per game) = (A + PO) / G

Batting Practice:
Introduction and Statistics

Numbers have always played a major role in baseball and its fans' love for the game. How many people can explain the significance of these numbers: 511; 73; 714; 56; .406; 4256?

Respectively, they represent Cy Young's career wins total; Barry Bonds's 2001 home run total; Babe Ruth's career home run total; the length in games of Joe DiMaggio's 1941 hitting streak; Ted Williams's 1941 batting average; Pete Rose's career hits total.

What is sabermetrics? The term is a combination of the acronym SABR (Society of American Baseball Research) and "metrics," meaning "measurement." Defined variously as the "search for objective knowledge about baseball" and "the mathematical and statistical analysis of baseball records" by the man who coined the term, noted baseball author Bill James, sabermetrics has become more and more widely accepted as an evaluation tool. Baseball fans, who already memorize and quote numbers to the thousandths place (as in no other part of their lives), now work into their baseball arguments such terms as OPS (on-base plus slugging percentages), its mathematically superior cousin, the SLOB (slugging times on base), WHIP (walks plus hits per inning pitched) and RF (range factor).

James once wrote that the main reason for sabermetrics is that there is a Baseball Hall of Fame, and sabermetrics arguments are frequently used to plead the case for a player's inclusion in (or exclusion from) the Hall. However, as Michael Lewis's bestseller *Moneyball* attests, baseball insiders are taking a serious look at sabermetrics as a team-building tool. Just as a study of baseball statistics can help people better understand mathematics, *Moneyball* is viewed in the business community as a model for business startups.

The main contribution of Bill James and Pete Palmer, another noted sabermetrician, is their exposure of the deficiency of looking at merely the traditional statistics. Fresh analysis can be provided by the new statistics, or at the very least, by a new twist on the old statistics.

When doing statistical analyses and data mining, anomalies are bound to appear, and baseball numbers are no stranger to these. For example, when combining unequally sized groups into a larger data set, expectations can be confounded. An example of this is known as Simpson's Paradox. To illustrate how this can work in baseball, consider the following example. Player A may have a .223 BA against right-handed pitching (45 H / 202 AB) and a .284 BA against lefties (71 H / 250 AB), giving him an overall BA of .257 (116 H / 452 AB). Player B may have a higher BA against righties (.232 on 58 H / 250 AB) and a higher one against lefthanders as well (.296 on 32 H / 108 AB), but his overall batting average can nonetheless be lower than that of player A (.251, or 90 H / 358 AB).

Descriptive statistics provide the mathematical underpinning for many of the measures used in sabermetrics, so it is here that we review some terms and formulas. If you feel comfortable with this subject, you may skip ahead to the next chapter.

Statistics Refresher

We define the *mean*, or average, of a data set to be the sum of the elements in the set divided by the total number of elements in the set. It is a measure of central tendency. Let's think about the mean by way of an example. The following are the year-by-year home run totals for Hank Aaron over the course of his career: 13 27 26 44 30 39 40 34 45 44 24 32 44 39 29 44 38 47 34 40 20 12 10. The mean of this set is denoted by the symbol $\bar{x}$ and is determined to be $\bar{x}$ = 32.83 (755 total home runs divided by 23 seasons). Another measure of central tendency is the *median*, which provides the midpoint of the data set. For Aaron's home runs, this is 34, i.e., he had as many seasons with more than 34 home runs as he did with fewer. Finally, the *mode* is the most frequently occurring element in the data set. For Aaron's home runs, this number is 44, which, coincidentally, also happens to be his uniform number. The mode and median are least affected by unusually high or low score, while the mean is most stable, meaning that it shows the least variability when several random samples are taken. In a data set that is normally distributed, one in which the data can be modeled by a bell-shaped curve, all three of the measures are equal. For Aaron, they are not; however, in his playing days, it would be reasonable to expect Hank Aaron to hit 32 to 34 home runs per season based on this data.

In statistics, measures of dispersion show how tightly spread out the data is in relation to a measure of central tendency. The main measures of the dispersion of the data are range, variance and standard deviation. Aaron's seasonal home run totals vary from a low of 10 to a high of 47. The *range* is the maximum minus the minimum, so for Aaron, this is 47 minus 10, or 37. If the home run data is broken up into quartiles, we see that the first quartile would be those values less than 26, the second quartile ends at the median (34) and the third quartile ends at 44. Thus, the interquartile range (IQR) is 44 − 26 = 18, meaning that 50 percent of the data is separated by 18.

A measure of dispersion that utilizes the mean is called the *variance*. Its formula is given by

$$s^2 = \frac{\sum (x_i - \bar{x})^2}{n-1}$$

where *n* represents the number of items in the data set. Aaron's season-by-season home run totals have a variance of 119.62. The square root of the variance is the *standard deviation*, and it is this measure that gives a clearer picture of the spread of the data. Aaron's standard deviation is 10.49, and it can be inferred from Chebyshev's rule that at least 75 percent of the data falls within two standard deviations of the mean, i.e., between 32.83 and ±(2 × 10.49) or between about 10 and 55, which in fact 100 percent of the values do.

The mathematical bases for many of the formulas used in sabermetrics are provided by a study of statistical regression and correlation. These studies attempt to determine a line that nearly approximates data that can be expressed as ordered pairs, and how well-defined this linear relationship is. If the second coordinate increases when the first coordinate does, then the correlation is said to be positive. If the second coordinate decreases when the first increases, the correlation is said to be negative. As an example, we will use a sample of the home run and runs batted in totals for some of the seasons of Gil Hodges' career. Hodges played 18 seasons in the National League, for the Brooklyn (and later Los Angeles) Dodgers and the New York Mets. Consider the following chart:

HR	11	23	32	40	32	31	42	27	32	27	22	25
RBI	70	115	113	103	102	122	130	102	87	98	64	80

Table 1.1 Gil Hodges' HR and RBI numbers for 12 years of his career

The data is entered point by point to create a picture called a *scatterplot*, and then we infer a curve or line that approximately passes through the points, which could then be used to predict second coordinates given a first coordinate. Here is the scatterplot for Hodges' home run and runs batted in data:

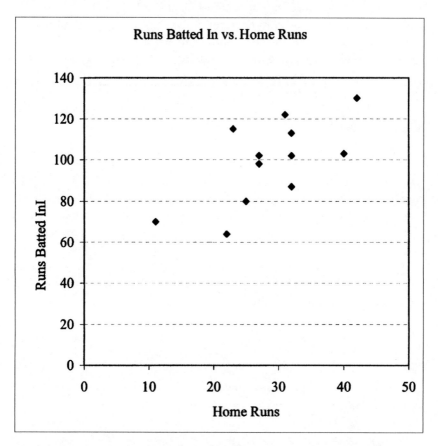

Figure 1.1 Scatterplot for Gil Hodges' 12 seasons of HR and RBI

It would seem that a line having positive slope would pass through the points, which would indicate a positive correlation. Obviously, a straight line could not possibly hit every point. Figure 1.2 shows the scatterplot with line segments connecting up all the points.

If we wanted to find a line to model this data in order to make some predictions, we would find that every x-value in the data set has a y-value associated with it that would not actually lie exactly on a line. We want to find a line that best fits the data. One common method of finding such a line is a process leading to a line in which the data points are shown to have

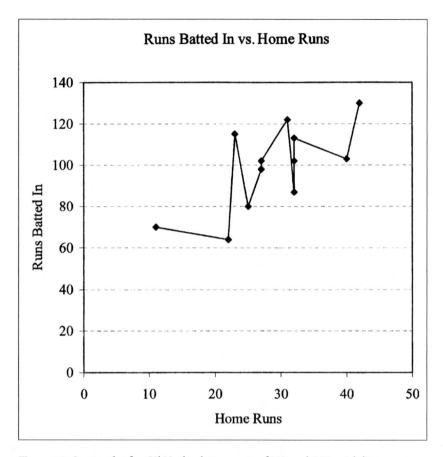

Figure 1.2 Scatterplot for Gil Hodges' 12 seasons of HR and RBI, with line segments joining the points

the minimum distance from it. Since the standard formula for distances involve square roots, a process in which the sum of the squares of the distances from the data points to their best fit line is called *the method of least squares*; the line is called *the least squares line*.

Recall that the slope-intercept equation for a line is generally represented as $y = mx + b$, where x represents the independent variable, y represents the dependent variable, m represents the *slope,* or the ratio of the difference between y-coordinates and the difference between their corresponding x-coordinates. The standard form for the least squares line is $y = ax + b$, where

$$a = \frac{n(\sum xy) - (\sum x)(\sum y)}{n(\sum x^2) - (\sum x)^2} \quad \text{and} \quad b = \frac{\sum y - a(\sum x)}{n}.$$

For Gil Hodges' home run and RBI data, these values are summarized in Table 1.2.

x	y	xy	x^2
11	70	770	121
22	64	1408	484
23	115	2645	529
25	80	2000	625
27	98	2646	729
27	102	2754	729
31	122	3782	961
32	87	2784	1024
32	102	3264	1024
32	113	3616	1024
40	103	4120	1600
42	130	5460	1764
344	1186	35249	10614

Table 1.2 Least squares computations for Gil Hodges' 12 seasons

By the formulas, a = 1.66, and b = 51.21, so the regression line has equation y = 1.66 x + 51.21. Thus, if Hodges had hit 35 home runs in the season, he would be expected to have 1.66 × 35 + 51.21 RBI, or roughly 109, not "dead-on" perfect, but not unreasonable in the context of his other seasons. To determine just how good the fit is, we compute the correlation coefficient r:

$$r = \frac{n(\sum xy) - (\sum x)(\sum y)}{\sqrt{n(\sum x^2) - (\sum x)^2} \; \sqrt{n(\sum y)^2 - (\sum y)^2}}$$

For this particular data set, the value of r is approximately 0.675. A value close to 1 indicates a high positive correlation, one close to −1 indicates a high negative correlation, and values close to zero mean a very weak correlation, or no correlation at all. Thus, Gil Hodges' home runs are moderately correlated with his RBI.

Infield Practice:
Sabermetrical Reasoning

Even though sabermetrics is defined as *the search for objective knowledge about baseball,* we must realize at the outset that the order of certainty in sabermetrics is nowhere near that of mathematics. To sabermetrically prove something means that a number of instruments (for example, runs created — see Inning 6: The Runs Created School) have been used to reinforce or strengthen a position, which, in turn, would make a conclusion plausible. But such a position should never be considered as permanently true as, for example, a proof of the Theorem of Pythagoras. There are just too many parameters and variables that Sabermetrics cannot take into account (see Seventh-Inning Stretch: Non-Sabermetrical Factors). In this chapter we illustrate how one might reason in a sabermetrical fashion, by way of an example which poses a number of questions which will be addressed throughout this book. We will not answer *all* the posed questions here; we will address them throughout the book as the relevant measures are presented.

In 1920, Babe Ruth hit 54 home runs, becoming the first player to slug thirty, forty and fifty home runs in a season. He also hit more home runs than every other American League team, and all but one of the National League clubs. A number of questions immediately arise:

- Was Ruth as dominant during any other year of his career?
- Did any of his contemporaries match his feat?
- Did any other slugger of any other era duplicate or surpass what Ruth did in 1920?

The first step is to look at the data. We see that, in addition to hitting such a heretofore unthinkable number of home runs, Ruth outdistanced the American League runner-up that season, fellow Hall of Famer George Sisler,

BABE RUTH HOME RUN TOTALS
VS. TEAM HOME RUN TOTALS, 1918–1933

YEAR	Ruth HR Total	Next Highest HR in ML	Difference between Ruth and Next	AL Teams Out-HRed by Ruth	NL Teams Out-HRed by Ruth
1918	11	11	0	4	1
1919	29	11	18	4	6
1920	54	19	35	7	7
1921	59	24	35	5	3(a)
1922	35	Suspended	—	1	1
1923	41	41	0	2(b)	1
1924	46	27	19	5	3
1925	25	Illness	—	—	—
1926	47	21	26	5	4
1927	60	47	13	7	5
1928	54	31	23	4	3
1929	46	43	3	2(c)	2
1930	49	Wilson/56	—	1	0
1931	46	46	0	3	3
1932	41	Foxx/58	—	1	0
1933	34	Foxx/48	—	0	0(d)

Table 2.1 Babe Ruth's seasonal home run totals (1918–1933)

by thirty-five home runs. Philadelphia Phillies' center fielder, Cy Williams, led the National League in 1920 with fifteen homers. How significant were these differences? One way to address this question is to compare other seasonal home run champions with their runners-up; we will use this relativity technique in future discussions.

Back to Ruth, we also find that he actually out-homered *pairs* of major league teams. For example, in 1920 the St. Louis Cardinals and the Cincinnati Reds hit fifty home runs between the two clubs, falling four short of Ruth's total. And there were ten other such pairs of teams that year. How significant was that? Did anybody else ever hit more home runs in a season than the combined total of two teams? If so, how many times? By all accounts, Ruth was a dominant force in 1920. Let us consider some other Ruthian years.

In Table 2.1, we consider sixteen of Babe Ruth's seasons. We look at his home run totals, from 1918 through 1933. We put these numbers into the context of the major leagues during that time span, comparing Ruth to his runner-up and also looking at the number of teams Ruth out-homered, season by season. It should be noted that during this period, Ruth won or tied for twelve home run crowns. We also point out that Ruth was suspended for six weeks in 1922 for ignoring the prohibition against barnstorming; this ban applied only to participants in the 1921 World Series. We note, too, that in 1925, Ruth spent a significant portion of the season out of the lineup due to illness. So, the Babe lost several games (or home run opportunities) during these two seasons. Finally, National Leaguer Hack Wilson led the major leagues with 56 home runs in 1930. Jimmie Foxx, of the American League, paced the major leagues in home runs during the 1932 and 1933 seasons.

(a) Tied Brooklyn Dodgers in 1921
(b) Tied Detroit Tigers in 1923
(c) Tied St. Louis Browns in 1929
(d) Tied Cincinnati Reds in 1933
Note that Ruth won the AL home run title in 1930.

SUMMARY:

Ruth out-homered major-league teams 90 times, excluding 4 ties
Ruth out-homered pairs of teams 18 times:

   1918 (1)   1920 (11)   1921 (3)   1927 (3)

So what can we make of this?

While much can be gleaned from this table, perhaps nothing is more telling than the dominance of Babe Ruth. We know *what* he did; in Sabermetrics, we ask "How can the significance of his performance over this sixteen-year period be measured?" Other questions follow, such as, "Was Ruth unique in what he accomplished?" Sabermetrical reasoning will assist us greatly in obtaining these answers. We give a table below which summarizes sabermetrical reasoning:

HOW TO REASON SABERMETRICALLY

- Carefully identify the question(s) or problem(s) to be discussed.
- Get all relevant information. With so many useful Web sites, the *data mining* involved should not be a difficult task.
- Use as many measures and instruments as possible.
- Use relativity and normalization arguments when comparing players of different eras.

- Exercise care with regard to:
  - Labels (e.g., HR / AB vs. AB / HR)
  - Definitions (e.g., ratio vs. differential)
  - Interpolation vs. Extrapolation
  - Projections
- Interpret the results. Do various approaches seem to converge to an objective conclusion?
- Consider the historical context with regard to technological developments, medical advances, etc.
- Consider any non-sabermetrical factors germane to the analysis.
- Realize the limitations of a sabermetrical proof.

Figure 2.2 Sabermetrical reasoning

Before we move on, however, there are many other factors which must be addressed. In Ruth's case, some of these include the fact that he did not play night games, that he never traveled by airplane on road trips and that he did not play against African-American opponents. These issues will be considered later on in the chapter Seventh Inning Stretch: Non-Sabermetrical Factors.

The Sultan of Swat held the career-home-run title from 1921 until 1974. The example above demonstrates how Babe Ruth's home run prowess can be sabermetrically reasoned to argue his dominance. Let's look at a pitching example. Suppose we wish to make an argument about the "magic number" of wins which will ensure a starting pitcher's election into Baseball's Hall of Fame. For decades, baseball players, writers, and fans would argue that 300 wins translates to a "lock" for admittance into Cooperstown. With most teams now employing a five-man starting rotation, is it possible any longer for a pitcher to win 300 games in his career? Let's establish a sabermetrical reasoning argument, according to our algorithm.

First, identify the question. "What is the career pitching victory total that should guarantee election for a pitcher into the Hall of Fame?" Maybe it will stay at 300 wins, but maybe not. Next, gather all the relevant information. Going to the World Wide Web, we need to gather information on those starting pitchers currently in the Hall and their victory totals. We also need to gather information on current (active) starting pitchers and seek to develop any trends, using as many measures as possible. Confining our search to starting pitchers, we find that there are 70 pitchers with a plaque in the Hall of Fame. Twenty-two of these have 300 or more career victories. Interestingly, all retired pitchers with at least 300 career victories are in the Hall of Fame (Greg Maddux is still active). Further, Bobby Mathews, who played 15 seasons from 1871 to 1887, ended his career with 297 victories, and he was *not* voted into the Hall of Fame.

What other measures or instruments should be introduced? Should we consider the average number of starts per season (for starters)? Cy Young pitched 22 years for the Cleveland Spiders (NL), St. Louis Cardinals (NL), Boston Americans (then Red Sox) (AL), and Cleveland Indians (AL), totaling 815 games started. His career total of 511 wins (and 316 losses) will probably never be equaled. In those 22 seasons, the Cyclone averaged just over 37 starts per season (even when 40 years old). He also averaged just over 23 wins per season. Walter "Big Train" Johnson is second on the all-time list with 417 career victories, all for the Washington Senators. In 21 seasons, he averaged close to 32 starts and almost 20 wins each season. One of the greatest left-handed starting pitchers of all time was Warren Spahn, who pitched for the Boston (and then Milwaukee) Braves. Spahnny had one fewer career start than the Big Train but garnered "only" 363 victories. One reason for this might be that he didn't begin really playing major league baseball until the age of 25, due to service in World War II. Over 21 seasons, he averaged just over 17 wins and 31 starts per season. Our sabermetrical reasoning should continue for every pitcher in the Hall of Fame. By examining the average number of starts and wins in a season, we can introduce some normalization into the study. By comparing these to other pitchers of their eras, or comparing their statistics to league averages, we could introduce the idea of relativity into the study. We could also explore the statistic of winning percentage (total wins divided by wins plus losses) or the notion of average wins per start. Cy Young had 511 wins / 815 starts = 0.627 wins per start. Or, looking at the reciprocal, Cy Young won a game every 1.59 starts (which really means that he won nearly two games every three games he started).

Roger Clemens, in comparison, had 354 victories at the end of the 2007 season, together with 707 career games started (he had one relief appearance during his 1984 rookie season). In 23 years, this translates to an average of 30 starts per season and just over 15 wins per season. If we multiply Clemens's average wins per start (0.500) times 49 starts, which is what Cy Young had in 1892 for the Spiders, we see that Clemens would win 24.5 games. Clemens has broken the 20-win plateau six times, with a career high of 24 in his third season, 1986. This is the point where we need to exercise caution with respect to extrapolation and prediction. Clemens never started more than 36 games in any of his 24 seasons. Why would we expect him to start 49 games, as Young did?

Now we look at the population of current starting pitchers. To get an unbiased population, we need to select those pitchers with a baseline of career starts or career victories, perhaps 100, 150, or 200. We do not want to be too restrictive. Next, interpret the results. Randy "Big Unit" Johnson had won 284 games in his 20-year career through the end of the 2007 season. He had also won five Cy Young Awards (and placed second three more times) as the best pitcher in his league. We can easily compute his average wins per season. Should his victory total be enough for the Hall of Fame? As a final example, consider the career of Greg "Mad Dog" Maddux. An amazing eighteen times in his 22-year career (through the 2007 season), Maddux won at least fifteen games in the season. That got him to the magic number of 300, and he has added to it every year, with 347 total victories. Perhaps we could determine how many other current pitchers have won at least fifteen games per season and could do it for 20 years (15 times 20 equals 300).

Here is where the historical context comes into play. Also, we might realize that our sabermetrical reasoning has some limitations. Perhaps non-sabermetrical factors now play a part. If you were voting for admittance into the Hall of Fame, how much weight would you put on a pitcher who pitched in fifteen All-Star games? With the recent role shifting of pitchers ("starters" give way to "set-up men" who then turn the game over to "closers"), and the fact that starting pitchers are currently averaging fewer innings per start than in earlier decades (which means close games might be decided after the starter has departed the game), our original question is not as trivial as initially suspected. If you can develop a sabermetrical argument that creates a new magic number of wins, several pitchers (and their agents) will suddenly be your best friends, while others will blame you for not getting a ticket to Cooperstown.

Fast Ball Down the Middle

Regarding home runs, has anyone in history been either as dominant or more dominant than Babe Ruth?

Curve Ball Low and Away

Who was the more dominant pitcher, Cy Young or Nolan Ryan? Consider both sabermetrical and non-sabermetrical factors.

Inning 1:
Simple Additive Formulas

While many sabermetrical formulas are rather complicated mathematical models, there are some that are very simple to compute, and can be used to compare players of different skills on a level playing field, i.e., they do not favor the high average hitter over the slugger, or vice versa. This first statistic, however, definitely favors the big power hitter.

On Base Plus Slugging and Batting Average (OPS + BA)

Most people are aware of OPS (see "Batting Practice" section) as a measure of offensive effectiveness, but the creator or creators of the POP™ Award (http://www.popaward.com/htdocs/index.htm) have come up with an extension of the formula to include batting average, calling it POP, which accumulates OPS and BA. Thus, if a player has a batting average of .300, an on-base percentage of .400, and a slugging percentage of .500, he would have POP = BA + OBA + SLG = .300 + .400 + .500 = 1.200. According to the POP™ Award Web site, 48 percent of the players who achieve one such season are enshrined in the Hall of Fame, and 71 percent of those with two or more such seasons, called "premier" seasons, are so honored.

In 1966, when he won the American League Most Valuable Player award while playing for the Baltimore Orioles, Frank Robinson had BA = .316, OBP = .410, and SLG = .637, so his POP was the sum of those figures — 1.363, one of five "premier" seasons in which he would have BA greater than .300, OBP greater than .400, and SLG greater than .500.

In 1954, when he was named National League Most Valuable Player while playing for the New York Giants, Willie Mays had a POP of 1.423, with BA = .345, OBP = .411, and SLG = .667, one of his four "premier" seasons.

HEQ–Offense

Michael Hoban was a professor of mathematics and dean at Monmouth University in New Jersey. He defined a formula to measure a batter's effectiveness, called the Hoban Effectiveness Quotient (HEQ): TB + R + RBI + SB + 0.5 × BB. Hoban stated that an HEQ of 600 represents an outstanding year at the bat. When evaluating players' careers, he looked at the average of the players' 10 best seasons of HEQ. In this way, he was measuring the consistency of a player's level of achievement over time.

The beauty of the formula lies in its simplicity; it is measure of how much business a player transacted in a given season. When he stole a record 130 bases in a single season (1982), Oakland outfielder Rickey Henderson scored an HEQ of 563. In that season, Henderson batted .267 and had an OPS of .780. The following table lists Henderson's offensive statistics:

	H	2B	3B	HR	R	RBI	SB	BB	HEQ
Henderson 1982	143	24	4	10	119	51	130	116	563

Table 3.1 Rickey Henderson's HEQ for 1982

To calculate his HEQ, we first need to determine Henderson's total bases (TB). The standard method of computing TB requires separating out the singles. Henderson had 143 hits. When we subtract the total number of non-singles from his hits (24 + 4 + 10 = 38), we get 143 − 38 = 105 singles. Thus, using the formula TB = Singles + (2 × Doubles) + (3 × Triples) + (4 × Home Runs), we obtain 105 + 2(24) + 3(4) + 4(10) = 205 total bases. This allows us to calculate Henderson's HEQ = TB + R + RBI + SB + 0.5 × BB = 205 + 119 + 51 + 130 + 0.5 × 116 = 563.

There is a shortcut that can be employed as well in the calculation of TB. Since the total number of hits is redundant in the double, triple and home run totals, TB can be calculated by reducing the weights on each of these figures by 1, and then adding the number of hits. Thus, instead of having a weight of 2, the doubles total is multiplied by 1, triples by 2 and home runs by 3: TB = H + Doubles + (2 × Triples) + (3 × Home Runs) = 143 + 24 + 2(4) + 3(10), which also equals 205.

During the same season, Milwaukee outfielder Gorman Thomas, co–HR champion, batted .245 with an OPS of .849. His HEQ was 540 (verifiable using the fact that his total bases were 287). Thomas's statistics for 1982 are listed in the following table:

	H	2B	3B	HR	R	RBI	SB	BB	HEQ
Thomas 1982	139	29	1	39	96	112	3	84	540

Table 3.2 Gorman Thomas' HEQ for 1982

A statistic such as HEQ can put players like Thomas and Henderson on a more or less equal footing as a basis of comparison, even though their skill sets were vastly different in 1982 (home run slugger versus all-time base stealer). HEQ is not recommended as a measure to compare players from different seasons.

There also is a defensive component for the HEQ, so from here on in, the offensive HEQ will be denoted HEQ-O, and the defensive component will be denoted HEQ-D.

HEQ–Defense

The defensive formula for HEQ is a bit more complicated, but it still is relatively easy to use. The fact is that, despite the disfavor into which fielding percentage has fallen among baseball researchers, there are not many ways to quantify defense.

Just like the HEQ-O formula, HEQ-D reflects the quantity of positive defensive plays. It is constructed as a different weighted formula for each defensive position, and the only raw data required is PO (putouts), A (assists), E (errors) and DP (double plays). All of these statistics are weighted, and each position has a Position Multiplication Factor (PMF) that adjusts the numbers in such a way that a season of 400 is considered outstanding. Pitchers are not measured using this statistic. Here are the HEQ-D formulas by position:

C: $(PO + 3 A + 2 DP \times 2 E) \times (0.445)$ [0.445 is PMF, and PO are capped at 800]

1B: $(0.25\ PO + 3A + DP - 2 E) \times (0.51)$ [0.51 is PMF]

2B, 3B, SS: $(PO + A + DP - 2 E) \times (PMF)$ [$PMF_{2b} = .46$, $PMF_{SS} = .548$, $PMF_{3b} = .888$]

OF: $(PO + 4 A + 4 DP - 2 E) \times (1)$ [i.e., no PMF for OF]

Let's calculate the HEQ for various players on the 2006 New York Mets team. First, consider the starting catcher, Paul LoDuca. He was credited with 802 PO, but the formula caps PO for catchers at 800 (catchers are credited with a PO whenever they hold onto the third strike in a strikeout), so he gets 800 PO. He had 59 A, was charged with 11 E, and participated in 4 DP. The PMF for catchers is .445. Thus, his HEQ-D for 2006 is

$$(PO + 3 A + 2 DP - 2 E) \times 0.445 =$$
$$[800 + 3(59) + 2(4) - 2(11)] \times 0.445 = 428.5$$

which is considered a fine defensive season.

At first base, Carlos Delgado had 1199 putouts, 70 assists, and participated in 94 double plays while committing 11 errors. The PMF for first basemen is .51, and we remark that, in the HEQ-D formula, only ¼ of the PO are counted, as many of the first baseman's PO are the result of routine throws from other infielders. Delgado's HEQ-D is (0.25 PO + 3 A +DP – 2 E) × 0.51 = [0.25(1199) + 3(70) + 94 – 2(11)] × 0.51 = 299.8, which, while not excellent, is in line with his defensive reputation.

In Table 3.3 we provide the HEQ-D for the top Mets starting players at each position.

2006 Mets	POS	PMF	PO	A	E	DP	HEQ-D
LoDuca	C	0.445	800*	59	11	4	428.5
Delgado	1B	0.51	1199	70	8	94	299.8
Valentin	2B	0.46	194	286	6	52	239.2
Wright	3B	0.888	107	288	19	30	343.7
Reyes	SS	0.548	176	390	17	71	330.4
Beltran	OF	none	357	13	2	6	411.0

Table 3.3 HEQ-D for the 2006 Mets players

Note that Beltran's defensive season falls into the "exceptional" category.

What Hoban does next is to add the HEQ-O and the HEQ-D to get a seasonal total. For Carlos Beltran, his offensive numbers for the HEQ-O are as follows:

	R	RBI	SB	BB	TB
Beltran	127	116	18	95	303

Table 3.4 Carlos Beltran's 2006 statistics

His HEQ-O = TB + R + RBI + SB + 0.5 × BB = 303 + 127 + 116 + 18 + 0.5(95) = 611.5, making his seasonal total HEQ-O + HEQ-D = 411 + 611.5 = 1022.5. This is overall an excellent season. In Hoban's analysis, the ten best seasons are averaged to obtain the Player Career Total (PCT). Ten seasons are chosen because Hall of Fame candidates need to have played for 10 years. As stated earlier, the average total HEQ for the player's ten best seasons is called the Player Career Total (PCT). A PCT of at least 830 seems to be a good indicator for Hall of Fame induction.

To test this indicator or boundary line, let's consider the career of Gil Hodges, first baseman for the Brooklyn Dodgers, who has received more votes for the Hall of Fame than any player in history, yet he has yet to be voted in as a member. His PCT is 904, based on the sum of his

HEQ-O and HEQ-D, rounded to the nearest whole number, for his 10 best seasons:

1954	*1951*	*1957*	*1950*	*1952*	*1953*	*1949*	*1955*	*1956*	*1958*	*AVG*
1056	1034	934	931	908	884	884	879	858	675	904

Table 3.5 Gil Hodges' PCT

The PCT values are sorted from highest to lowest for the ten best seasons, which run from 1949 to 1958 consecutively.

Total Average

Another rather simple measure to use and understand is Total Average (TA). Popularized and conceived by Washington Post baseball writer Thomas Boswell, the statistic is essentially a ratio between a player's bases gained and outs made. In fact, it is similar in form to Barry Codell's Base-Out-Percentage (BOP). First we provide the formulas, and then we will analyze them:

Total Average = (TB + BB + HBP + SB) / (AB − H + SH + SF + CS + GIDP)
BOP = (TB + BB + HBP + SB + SH + SF) / (AB − H + SH + SF + CS + GIDP).

Note that the denominators are precisely the same — the number of outs that can be credited to the batter. The GIDP (Grounded Into Double Play) is counted again because the batter has caused two outs, and one of those is counted in AB − H. The BOP includes the number of sacrifices in the numerator, the base portion, because they always result in a runner advancing a base. Look again at Rickey Henderson's 1982 season:

AB	*H*	*2B*	*3B*	*HR*	*R*	*RBI*	*SB*	*CS*	*BB*	*HBP*	*SH*	*SF*	*GIDP*
536	143	24	4	10	119	51	130	42	116	2	0	2	5

Table 3.6 Rickey Henderson's 1982 offensive statistics

Applying the above formulas, we find that his TA = 1.0249, and his BOP = 1.0294. Note that his BOP is almost identical to his TA, in part because he had no sacrifice bunts and only 2 sacrifice flies.

Boswell asserts that any Total Average over 1.000 is "fantastic" because the player "gets more bases than he makes outs," while more than .900 indicates star or superstar level, .800 indicates all-star level, and everyday players are clustered in the .700s. Boswell also states that the comparisons work best for players within the same league and the same season, and that the vagaries of offense from era to era are a factor. Only two players who were active during the so-called Deadball Era had career TA over 1.000 (Ty Cobb and Tris Speaker).

To bring the stat into focus, an element of relativity can be introduced. The past league statistics do not always have sacrifice fly (SF) totals available, so they have been left out of the calculation. In 1982, the American League had an aggregate TA = 0.655. The league SF was not available at *Baseball-reference.com,* so it was obtained from the *Stats Inc. All-Time Baseball Sourcebook.* Thus, the player's TA relative to his league can be computed by taking TA / League TA, which for Rickey Henderson in 1982 was 1.025 / 0.655 = 1.554. This indicates that his TA was about 55 percent better than that of the average player in 1982.

In 1915, Ty Cobb stole 96 bases. Sacrifice flies and grounded into double plays statistics are not available for that season, so they will be eliminated from the TA computation. Here is the raw data:

AB	H	2B	3B	HR	R	RBI	SB	CS	BB	HBP	SH
563	208	31	13	3	144	99	96	38	57	6	9

Table 3.7 Ty Cobb's 1915 offensive statistics

Cobb's TA is (TB + BB + HBP + SB) / (AB − H + SH + SF + CS + GIDP) = (274 + 57 + 6 + 96) / (563 − 208 + 9 + 0 + 38 + 0) = 1.077. This is slightly higher than that of Henderson, but when relativity is factored into the equation, the difference is much starker. Here are the numbers for the American League in 1915, with SF and GIDP unavailable:

AB	H	2B	3B	HR	R	SB	CS	BB	HBP	SH
40304	10005	1409	617	160	4922	1443	1051	4217	969	1074

Table 3.8 American League offensive statistics for 1915

As we know, the Deadball Era was a low time for offense. The 1915 American League Total Average is 0.609 (verify this), and so, for Cobb, (TA) / (League TA) = 1.077 / 0.609 is 1.77, which means that he was 77 percent better than the average American League player in 1915. Thus, while Cobb's raw Total Average is slightly higher than that of Henderson, put into the context of their respective leagues, Cobb's season was significantly better.

Easy Tosses

1. Through the 2006 season, Barry Bonds had career marks in BA, OBP, and SLG, respectively, of .299, .443, and .608. Calculate his career POP.

2. Ryan Howard and Justin Morneau won their respective league's Most Valuable Player award in 2006, and Albert Pujols was a strong contender for the National League award. Their numbers were:

	BA	*OBP*	*SLG*
Pujols	.331	.431	.671
Howard	.313	.425	.659
Morneau	.321	.375	.559

Calculate the POP for each.

3. The 2006 World Champion St. Louis Cardinals had the following raw offensive numbers for the top starting player at each position:

	POS	*R*	*RBI*	*SB*	*BB*	*H*	*2B*	*3B*	*HR*
Molina	C	29	49	1	26	90	26	0	6
Pujols	1B	119	137	7	92	177	33	1	49
Miles	2B	48	30	2	38	112	20	5	2
Rolen	3B	94	95	7	56	154	48	1	22
Eckstein	SS	68	23	7	31	146	18	1	2
Edmonds	OF	52	70	4	53	90	18	0	19

Calculate the HEQ-O for each player.

4. The 2006 World Champion St. Louis Cardinals had the following raw defensive numbers for the top starting player at each position:

	POS	*PO*	*AS*	*E*	*DP*
Molina	C	736	77	4	6
Pujols	1B	1345	110	6	145
Miles	2B	165	232	10	58
Rolen	3B	93	318	15	32
Eckstein	SS	178	363	6	87
Edmonds	OF	223	4	3	0

Using the proper PMF, calculate the HEQ-D for each player.

5. Using the numbers computed in questions 3 and 4 above, calculate the PMT for each of the Cardinals starting players from 2006.

6. Calculate the TA for Pujols and Howard given the raw data below:

	AB	H	2B	3B	HR	R	RBI	SB	CS	BB	HBP	SH	SF	GIDP
Pujols	535	177	33	1	49	119	137	7	2	92	4	0	3	20
Howard	581	182	25	1	58	104	149	0	0	108	9	0	6	7

Hard Sliders

1. The American League in 1966 had a BA of .240, OBP of .306 and SLG of .369, while the 1954 NL numbers were .265, .335, and .407, respectively. Using the POP calculated in this chapter for Willie Mays and Frank Robinson, calculate their relative POP.

2. Barry Bonds's 2001 season at bat is often compared to Babe Ruth's season in 1921 for sheer dominance. Below are their numbers for the year, coupled with their league's numbers:

	AB	H	2B	3B	HR	SB	CS	BB	HBP	SH
Bonds 2001	476	156	32	2	73	13	3	177	9	0
NL 2001	88100	23027	4613	488	2952	1456	735	8567	969	1074
Ruth 1921	540	204	44	16	59	17	13	145	4	4
AL 1921	42829	12525	2140	694	477	685	545	3965	301	1528

Some interesting observations about the chart

• The 2001 NL had exactly twice the number of teams as did the AL in 1921;
• The AL in 1921 batted a robust .292, while the NL in 2001 batted .261;
• The number of home runs and triples make for an interesting comparison, as do the number of sacrifice bunts (SH) and caught stealing (CS), all of which point to the different styles of play in these two leagues.

Calculate the TA for Ruth and Bonds, and their respective leagues, and then compute their relative TA. Note that the SF and GDP data, while available for NL 2001 and the two players, is not available for the AL in 1921. Thus, these quantities should be left out for all the computations in this problem.

3. Can the POP, TA and HEQ be combined in some way to form a new statistic that measures all-around play? Come up with such a statistic, and use it to compare Rickey Henderson and Gorman Thomas in 1982, and Albert Pujols and Ryan Howard in 2006.

Formulas

HEQ-O (Hoban Effectiveness Quotient–Offense) = TB + R + RBI + SB + 0.5 (BB)

HEQ-D (Hoban Effectiveness Quotient–Defense): Based on defensive position (note — none for Pitcher)

C: (PO + 3A + 2 DP − 2 E) × (0.445) [0.445 is PMF, and PO are capped at 800]

1B: (0.25 PO + 3A + DP − 2 E) × (0.51) [0.51 is PMF]

2B, 3B, SS: (PO + A + DP − 2 E) × (PMF) [PMF_{2b} = .46, PMF_{ss} = .548, PMF_{3b} = .888]

HEQ = HEQ-O + HEQ-D

PCT (Player Career Total): Average HEQ over 10 best seasons

TA (Total Average) = (TB + BB + HBP + SB) / (AB − H + SH + SF + CS + GIDP)

BOP (Base-Out-Percentage) = (TB + BB + HBP + SB+ SH + SF) / (AB − H + SH + SF + CS + GIDP)

Relative {stat}= (Player {stat})/(League {stat})

Inning 2: Peak versus Career Performances

In *The Bill James Historical Baseball Abstract,* the author compares and contrasts great players in many ways, using a number of sabermetrical measures to rank performances of Hall of Famers and All-Stars. One way James rates players is to consider their peak performances: statistics covering roughly a four- or five-year period in which the player posted his best statistics, the years not necessarily being consecutive. James also evaluates performances by considering how players performed throughout their careers, looking at, among other things, their accumulated statistical totals.

In this chapter we offer a systematic way to consider both types of performances. We note that evaluating the peak performance of an individual necessitates comparing him with his contemporaries. How one star performed relative to other stars of his era, may shed some light in comparing players of different times. In a sense, when looking at career ratings, one might only consider the players' bottom-line career totals. However, it is important to put these numbers into proper context, historical and otherwise, when ranking the great players, past and present. This issue will be addressed in the chapter *Seventh-Inning Stretch: Non-Sabermetrical Factors.*

There is a certain amount of subjectivity here, especially with regard to the selection of "peak" years. In the two figures below, we suggest methodologies to determine both peak and career values.

SOME CONSIDERATIONS IN DETERMINING "PEAK" VALUE

- Determine the player to be considered.
- Determine the player's range of ages during the years under consideration. The span of years will generally, but not always, be four to six years, and will rarely include ages younger than 25 or older than 35.

- After obtaining appropriate data, determine what hitting, fielding and/or pitching measures will be used in the analysis.
- Consider all players with rivaling statistics, players in the same or different eras.
- Strive to answer the following questions:
  - How dominant was the player in his era during these peak years?
  - Was anyone else approximately as dominant in the same or different eras?
- Finally, did the player contribute to his team(s) winning divisional, league or world titles in any significant way?
- Formulate the results. Can the players under consideration be ranked in any objective way giving plausible conclusions? What about non-sabermetrical factors?

Figure 4.1. Determining "peak" value

SOME CONSIDERATIONS IN DETERMINING TOP CAREER VALUE

- Determine the players to be considered.
- After obtaining the career data, determine what hitting, fielding and/or pitching measures will be used in the analysis.
- Consider all players with rivaling statistics.
- Strive to answer the following questions:
  - How dominant was the player vis-à-vis any other player in history? Do his statistics represent an anomaly in any way?
  - Was anyone else approximately as dominant in the same or different eras?
- Finally, did the player contribute to his team(s) winning divisional, league or world titles in any significant way? Was he considered an all-around star in his era?
- Formulate the results. Can the players under consideration be ranked in any objective way giving plausible conclusions? What about non-sabermetrical factors?

Figure 4.2. Determining "career" value

A player like Lou Gehrig, for instance, would have an extremely high peak value. In fact, over a ten year period, from 1927 through 1936, Gehrig's production is nearly unrivaled. Due to his premature retirement, his career value is perhaps not as dominant, but it would be difficult to choose any other first baseman in history with greater career statistics.

Another argument for comparing peak versus career values has to do with the pinnacle of a player's career, gaining entrance into the National Baseball Hall of Fame. Are there certain numbers which automatically qualify a player for the Hall? In the 1980s, if a player ended his career with 500 home runs or 3000 base hits or 300 pitching victories, most folks would say he was a lock for Cooperstown. The career totals for ballplayers would almost guarantee enough votes. Is this true today? Or, similarly, if a player has a fantastic peak season, relative to other players, is that enough to warrant a plaque in Cooperstown? We offer a few examples.

Let's consider some offensive examples first. Roger Maris will always be known as the player who broke Babe Ruth's single-season mark for total home runs. Of course, every argument about the 1961 season includes the notion that Maris' Yankees played eight more games (162) than Ruth's Yankees (154). Let's contrast Roger Maris' peak and career totals. In 1961, Roger played in 161 games. In 590 at-bats, he led the American League in runs (with 132), in home runs (with 61) and in runs batted in (with 142). His batting average was .269, his on-base percentage was .372, and his slugging percentage was .620. Does this qualify for a peak season? Roger was coming off of a good season in 1960, where he led the league in slugging (with .581) and RBI (with 112). He was named an outfielder on the Sporting News Major League All-Star Team in 1960, won a Gold Glove as right fielder that year, and won the league's Most Valuable Player Award. He also hit 39 home runs, but that did not lead the league.

In 1961, however, his offensive numbers improved. He again won the MVP award for the American League, was named to the Sporting News AL All-Star Team, and he was named Major League Player of the Year by the *Sporting News*. His runs scored, hits, home runs, RBI, walks, hit-by-pitch, sacrifice flies, on-base percentage, and slugging percentage were all career highs. Never before, and never again, would his offensive statistics measure up to those of 1961. We could argue that his peak season was in 1961.

How did that season compare to other sluggers in the American League? We don't need to go much further than Roger's own Yankees. Most fans know that Maris was battling Mickey Mantle all season for the home run crown. In 1961, Mantle played in 153 games (eight fewer than Maris). The Mick also scored 132 runs, but he had 163 hits, compared to Rajah's 159. Mantle hit 54 homers and knocked in 128 runs, but he had 126 walks to lead the league, had 12 stolen bases (to Maris' zero) and led the AL in slugging with a .687 mark. Finally, Mantle batted .317, second to teammate Elston Howard's .348. Mantle also hit more home runs in 1960 than Maris (40).

Recall that some of the questions that we strive to answer are: How dominant was the player in his era during these peak years? And was anyone else approximately as dominant in the same or different eras?

During his peak, Maris was a good ballplayer. Perhaps it's unfair to judge him, as he played on the Yankees, who were always under intense scrutiny. Back to our peak criteria, did the player contribute to his team winning league or world titles in any significant way? In the 1960 World Series, in 25 at-bats, Mantle batted .400 and slugged .800, with three home runs and eleven runs batted in. In 1960, Roger Maris batted .267, slugged .500, with two home runs and two runs batted in in his 30 at-bats. A year later, the new home run king batted .105 in the Series, with one homer and two RBIs, while Mantle batted .167 (recall that he was injured and played in limited duty — two games). Maris had a peak season in 1961, but in comparison to other players and using the criteria outlined above, his peak was not as significant as others in his era.

Eddie Murray gained induction to the Hall of Fame in 2003, after playing 21 seasons and amassing over 11,000 at-bats in 3036 games. The amazing part about Eddie's career is that he never had a "peak" season; he was consistent throughout his career. He hit 504 home runs and batted in 1917 runs. He had 3255 base hits. His career batting average was .287 and his career slugging percentage was .476. He averaged 27 home runs in a season, but the most he ever hit was 33 in 1983. That was the year the Orioles won the World Series and, incidentally, 33 was Murray's jersey number. He averaged 103 RBIs per season, yet his highest output was 124 (in 1985). Eddie Murray was voted American League Rookie of the Year in 1977, was voted to only eight All-Star teams, and placed in the top ten in league Most Valuable Player Award voting eight times, never winning (although he did place second in 1982 and 1983). Could it be that Eddie Murray was inducted because his career totals eclipsed the "magic numbers" of 500 home runs and 3000 hits? When Murray retired, he was 15th on the career home run total list. At the end of the 2007 season he was 23rd, and the five players who passed him may not "automatically" be inducted into the Hall of Fame simply on the basis of their more than 500 career homers.

Don Sutton's record would indicate that he was more valuable over his career than during any peak seasons. The Hall of Fame pitcher won 324 games, yet only broke the seasonal twenty-victory mark once, in 1976 when he had 21 wins. At the end of 2007, Roger Clemens, Greg Maddux and Tom Glavine were the only pitchers who have pitched in the last fifteen years to have won more than 300 career games. Does this suggest that truly great future pitchers will never win 300 games in their career? Except for strike-shortened seasons, someone had always won at least 20 games in a season until 2006, when the National League leader had 16 (six pitchers tied for the league lead) and the American League leader had 19 (two pitchers). The league leaders in games started for the past several seasons are averaging 34 or 35 starts, and not every starting pitcher gets a decision in every game. Further, with today's specialty pitchers (relievers, one-out match-up pitchers, closers, etc.), starters are averaging fewer than six innings per start and many games are decided after the starter has departed for the showers. So racking up an average of 15 wins in a season for a twenty-year career (15 × 20 = 300) seems to indicate that we might not see a 300-game winner again for a very long time.

Many Hot Stove League conversations are fueled with "Peak versus Career" arguments. For example, who was the more valuable pitcher, Sandy Koufax or Don Sutton?

We have considered the peak versus career value for both hitters and pitchers. We could extend this notion to fielders as well, although most general managers want "complete position players"; GMs want a player who can both field and hit for average. Gone are the days when a player was in the line-up solely for his glove. Hall of Fame manager Earl Weaver once remarked that saving a run is as important as scoring a run, a sentiment that displayed his appreciation of Gold Glove players who might not always hit for power or average (Mark Belanger or Paul Blair). Rod Carew is in the Hall of Fame for his hitting (3053 career hits), yet his 33 errors at second base in 1974 were the most ever by a second baseman since 1946. His fielding percentage was .015 below the league average, but his batting average was .101 above the league mean.

Hitting, pitching, and fielding are individual talents. Can the peak-value analysis be applied to teams? Teams win games by scoring more runs than their opponents. Maybe Weaver's remark is noteworthy in this regard. At the end of a 154-game or 162-game season, did the team who scored the highest number of runs win the pennant? Or, did the team with the most victories prevail and capture the World Series trophy? Can we use the considerations of Figure 4.1 and apply them to teams? (For more on the relationship of runs scored and runs allowed to wins and losses, see Inning 4: The Linear Weights School — Offense).

The first part of the process is to determine which teams to study. Suppose we look at some teams that have been labeled "dynasties"—those teams that went to the World Series at least three years in a row. Maybe they didn't win the series all three years, but they played on the big stage for the opportunity. The New York Yankees immediately come to mind (1921–1923, 1936–1939, 1949–1953, 1960–1964, and 1998–2001). Wow! Also, the Chicago Cubs (1906–1908), the New York Giants (1921–1924), the Philadelphia Athletics (1929–1931), the St. Louis Cardinals (1942–1944), the Baltimore Orioles (1969–1971), and the Oakland Athletics (1972–1974 and 1988–1990). Our analysis could determine if these teams exhibited a peak value during their stretch of appearances in the Fall Classic. One drawback of such a study, however, is the homogeneity of the data. In how many cases were the teams fielding the same roster (with the same output) year after year? Were free agents brought into the mix? Were trades a major part of the championship? Perhaps we need to analyze individual teams and compare them to various eras.

In 2004, the Boston Red Sox fielded a powerful offensive team en route to the World Championship. The next year, the Sox brought back much of the same team, yet they failed to win the American League pennant. Should sabermetricians consider 2004 a peak season for Boston, and how does it compare to the peaks of other Boston teams? What measures should we use? Should we limit the study to just the number of victories? The number of runs scored? Runs allowed?

Let's gather some data (initially look at simple statistics—team batting average and earned run average). We should also take relativity into account, as we compare the Boston Red Sox of 2004 to the 1986 Red Sox, the 1975 Red Sox, the 1946 Red Sox, and the 1918 Red Sox. (Incidentally, the Boston Americans / Red Sox won five World Series titles from 1901 through 1918, the last three with a young left-handed pitching sensation named Ruth). In Table 4.1, we show the BA, ERA, Average Runs Scored (RS) and Average Runs Allowed (RA) for these five Boston teams, as well as the league batting average and ERA (the runs scored and runs allowed averages for the league are the same).

	BA	ERA	RS	RA	Lg BA	Lg ERA	Lg RS/RA
2004	.282	4.18	5.86	4.74	.270	4.63	5.01
1986	.271	3.93	4.93	4.32	.262	4.17	4.61
1975	.275	3.98	4.98	4.43	.258	3.78	4.30
1946	.271	3.38	5.08	3.81	.256	3.50	4.06
1918	.249	2.31	3.76	3.02	.254	2.77	3.64

Table 4.1 **Boston Red Sox team statistics**

Which was the best Boston Red Sox team? Which team had the best peak value? Only the 1918 team had a lower-than-the-league batting average. Obviously, we would need to study more than just team batting average, ERA and runs scored or allowed. Keep in mind that in 1918 and 1946, pitchers' batting statistics were incorporated into the team average in the American League. Look at the difference between runs scored and runs allowed for the Ted Williams 1946 team. In addition, non-sabermetrical factors might be incorporated. Finally, despite all of the statistics, only the 1918 and 2004 teams brought the championship home to Boston. How does that factor into the analysis? This example should provide an idea of how to conduct a relativity argument for teams. (By the way, where would the 2007 Red Sox fit in?)

An Inside Pitch

Consider the peak seasons of Barry Bonds, Mark McGwire and Sammy Sosa. Which one of these three sluggers had the best peak value with regard to home runs?

An Outside Pitch

Compare the career values of the following batting champions: Ty Cobb, Harry Heilmann, Stan Musial and Tony Gwynn.

A Fork Ball

The following pitchers have not yet been elected to the Hall of Fame, but each has more than 250 career victories. Compare their career values: Tommy John, Bert Blyleven, Jim Kaat, and Jack Morris.

An Intentional Walk

Compare the peak value of the Pittsburgh Pirates teams of 1990, 1991, and 1992. Use the following measures: RS, RA, ERA, BA, OBP, SLG. Which was the best team? These three teams won 96, 98, and 95 games, respectively, easily winning their division. However, all three teams lost in the National League Championship Series. Any ideas why?

Hit and Run

In a 162-game season, does the team that scores the most runs win the pennant? Compare the team peak value for the following teams, given their win-loss record, runs scored, runs allowed, and finish: the 1998 New York Yankees, 2001 Seattle Mariners, and the 2003 Atlanta Braves. What conclusions can you draw?

Inning 3:
The Equivalence Coefficient

"What if...?"

This question has fueled baseball discussions for decades. For example, in the 1937 All-Star Game, twenty-seven-year-old Cardinal right-hander Dizzy Dean was hit in the foot by Cleveland outfielder Earl Averill's line drive, suffering a broken toe. This injury subsequently caused him to alter his pitching motion, and Dean was never the dominant pitching force he had been. What if this had not happened? What would the record book show if Dean's career had tapered off "naturally"?

Another example can be made by considering the career of Hank Greenberg. The Tiger first baseman was a contemporary of both Jimmie Foxx and Lou Gehrig. (Can you imagine any opposing pitcher facing three more dominant first basemen at any other time in history?) Greenberg drove in 183 runs in 1937 and slugged 58 home runs the following year. He was probably on his way to amassing career numbers which would have approached those of Babe Ruth when in 1941, he appeared in only nineteen games, The next time he suited up was in 1945 when, at the age of 34, he played in 78 games. This was due to the fact that Greenberg responded to the call to serve his country during World War II. One wonders what he would have accomplished had he, like Ted Williams (see below), not missed well over four seasons.

In this chapter we attempt to answer questions related to the two examples just given, by the development of an instrument which we call the *equivalence coefficient* (EC). Before the advent of sabermetrics, individual pitching statistics were pretty much limited to wins versus losses, winning percentage, earned run average and strikeouts. And individual fielding was usually assessed by computing the number of putouts, assists and errors made by a fielder. While this is no longer the case, there were more hitting statistics than those involving pitching and fielding measures in the past, and the same is true *today*. It is because of this that we will begin our discussion with batting.

By the very nature of the game of baseball, a team must score at least one run to win a game. No team has ever won a game by the score of 0–0. Hitting has captured the hearts of many fans throughout the years. Imagine seeing the Flying Dutchman, Honus Wagner, scorching a line drive. Picture Stan Musial slashing a double. Watch as Mickey Mantle reaches the ancient green façade at Yankee Stadium. Recall Willie Mays circling the bases. Remember Hank Aaron completing one of his 755 home runs. Visualize Pete Rose's single which surpassed Ty Cobb's lifetime total of hits. Cobb won twelve batting titles in thirteen years. Rogers Hornsby averaged .402 over a five-year stretch. Lou Gehrig slugged twenty-three grand slam home runs.

Hitting. It has consumed us, right up through these past years of the McGwire-Sosa-Bonds home run explosion. All of the players mentioned above, and scores of others were (or are) great hitters. But we will now ask a "What if?" question. This, in turn, will provide impetus for the idea of the EC.

Two of the national pastime's most famous hitters were Ted Williams and Babe Ruth. Many have argued quite convincingly that one or the other was the greatest hitter ever. Williams' career spanned four decades (1939–1960) and Ruth's twenty-two-year career went from 1914 until 1935. As great as their records were, however, their at-bats totals were relatively small: Ruth batted about 8400 times; Williams approximately 7700 times. Even when their base on balls totals are brought into the discussion (over 2000 for both sluggers), the number of times they each appeared at the plate pales in comparison to other great hitters. Williams was called into the armed forces twice: for World War II and during the Korean War. Ruth began his career as a pitcher, not playing every day; he also lost time due to suspensions (for example, in 1922 and 1925) and to illness (1925). In contrast, Pete Rose batted over 14,000 times and Hank Aaron had well over 12,000 at-bats.

Williams and Ruth were not the only ones with a lower-than-expected number of plate appearances; others, for one reason or another, had a similar fate. For example, Ruth's teammate, Yankee legend Lou Gehrig, died before he reached the age of thirty-eight. Hall of Famer Sandy Koufax retired before his thirty-first birthday. And All-Star Don Mattingly will most probably be denied entrance into the Hall of Fame primarily because of his diminished career totals, brought on by a chronic back injury which led to his premature retirement. One wonders how the records of these three individuals — and many more — would read if their careers had been extended.

Returning to Williams and Ruth, we ask the following question: "Although they posted great numbers, can we speculate about or predict — in any reasonable way — what numbers they might have accumulated, given more hitting opportunities? Is there a plausible way to project or estimate what might have been, given different circumstances?

Specifically, we will attempt to answer three questions:

- *What would Williams' totals have been had he not lost so much time?*
- *What if Ruth had not started out as a pitcher?*
- *Who was the greater hitter: Williams or Ruth?*

To give us a starting point regarding these questions, we consider the table below, which gives some of the career totals for both Hall of Famers (see Pre-Game: Abbreviations and Formulas at the beginning of this book for definitions):

Statistic	Williams	Ruth
At Bats (AB)	7706	8398
Hits (H)	2654	2873
Walks (BB)	2021	2062
Runs (R)	1798	2175
Runs Batted In (RBI)	1839	2217
Home Runs (HR)	521	714
Total Bases (TB)	4884	5793
Batting Average (BA)	.344	.342
Slugging Average (SLG)	.634	.690
Isolated Power (ISO)	.290	.348
Power Factor (PwrF)	1.843	2.018
Total Power Quotient (TPQ)	0.940	1.039

Table 5.1 Williams versus Ruth — lifetime totals

To attempt to answer these questions, we will make three assumptions:

(1) Let us suppose that both Williams and Ruth had, for the sake of argument, 12,500 plate appearances (PA). By a plate appearance we mean either an AB or a BB, neglecting both sacrifices and being hit by a pitch, since these numbers are relatively small compared to PA.

(2) Furthermore, let us assume that their respective additional ABs are to be determined by preserving the ratio of AB to PA.

(3) Finally, let's introduce a special factor. Let us assume that Williams would have been 5% better for his time missed, since these years were prime years. As an added scenario, we will also assume that he would have been 10% better. At the same time, since Ruth pitched early in his career, we will suppose that for his added AB he would have been 5% less the hitter he was during the latter years of his career.

Let's start with Ruth. From the table above, we see that the Babe had 8398 AB and 2062 BB for a total of 10,460 PA. Hence, if x is the number of additional AB, the following proportion preserves the AB to PA ratio:

$$\frac{8398}{8398+2062}=\frac{8398+x}{12500}$$

To solve this equation for x, we merely "cross multiply" and isolate the unknown quantity to obtain $x = 1638$. So Ruth would get an additional 1638 AB. This implies that he would also receive an additional 402 BB, because 8398 AB + 1638 (additional AB) + 2062 BB + 402 (additional BB) = 12,500 PA.

So, if Ruth was just as good as he always was for these extra 1638 AB, then his projected HR total would be:

$$714+\frac{1638}{8393}(714)=714+139=853$$

We note that the term

$$\frac{1638}{8393}(714)$$

is nothing more than a prorating of the 714 statistic. But we are assuming that Ruth would be 5 percent *less* the hitter he was during the rest of his career. Therefore, the

$$\frac{1638}{8393}(714)=139$$

term should be multiplied by 0.95, giving the true projected HR figure as:

$$714+\frac{1638}{8393}(714)(0.95)=714+132=846$$

Note that the left-hand side of this last equation has a "714" in both terms. If we factor out the 714 (and recall that the number "1" is always an understood coefficient of any term), we see that

$$714(1+\frac{1638}{8398}(0.95))=714(1+0.185)=714(1.185)=846$$

In other words, if we multiply 714 by the coefficient 1.185, we get the projected cumulative HR total for Babe Ruth.

We call this the *equivalence coefficient*, because it gives us a "reasonable" estimate of the desired cumulative HR total, given our defined "equivalent" scenario.

With regard to Ted Williams, his additional AB compute to 2197, while his additional BB come to 576. Using the 5 percent better and 10 percent better assumptions (giving kickers of 1.05 and 1.10, respectively), we find that the equivalence coefficients for Williams are 1.299 and 1.314, respectively. So, a 5 percent better Williams would hit 521(1.299) = 677 HR, while a 10 percent better Williams would project to 521(1.314) = 685 HR.

We summarize the technique of computing the EC in Figure 5.1.

HOW TO COMPUTE THE EQUIVALENCE COEFFICIENT (EC) FOR BATTING

- Determine the projected or desired number of new PA.

- Form the following proportion: $\dfrac{AB}{AB + BB} = \dfrac{AB + x}{New\ PA}$

- Solve for x; this will give the additional number of AB.

- $EC = 1 + \dfrac{x}{AB}(k)$, where k is the kicker. Note that $k > 1$, if the player is assumed to be better during the additional AB; $k < 1$, if the player is assumed to be worse during the additional AB. Finally, if $k = 1$, we are essentially prorating his statistics based on past performances.

- Multiply the EC by the desired cumulative statistic, to get a projected total. This applies to RBI, HR, etc.

- Note that the EC is not applied to relative statistics in the same way. For example, to find an equivalent BA, one must first compute the projected H, then divide this by the projected AB.

Figure 5.1 Computing the equivalence coefficient for batting

We see that the equivalence coefficient has enabled us to compile the entries in the following table, perhaps shedding some light to answer the questions we posed above:

- *What would Williams' totals be if he had not lost so much time?*
- *What if Ruth had not started out as a pitcher?*
- *Who was the greater hitter: Williams or Ruth?*

Projected Totals	Williams (+5%)	Williams (+10%)	Ruth (-5%)
EC	1.229	1.314	1.185
AB	9903	9903	10336
H	3448	3487	3405
BB	2597	2597	2464
R	2336	2363	2577
RBI	2389	2416	2627
HR	677	685	846
TB	6344	6418	6865
BA	.348	.352	.339
SLG	.641	.648	.684
ISO	.293	.296	.345
PwrF	1.842	1.841	1.983
TPQ	0.951	0.961	1.020

Table 5.2 Williams versus Ruth using the equivalence coefficient

So, who *was* the greater hitter?

Some remarks are in order regarding this approach. First, the EC can be regarded as a mathematical model. As with most models, it can be tweaked. For example, we assumed that Ted Williams was "equally better" during the years he missed in both the 1940s and in the 1950s. We could have assumed that he was 10 percent better in the 1940s and 5 percent better in the 1950s. Clearly, this would have yielded different projections and made our model a bit more complicated (see the *Hard Slider* problem at the end of the chapter).

We also assumed that the proportions of AB to PA were constant. But if Williams was 10 percent better in the 1940s, perhaps he would have been even more selective regarding what pitches to hit, meaning that he might have had less than a total of 9903 AB, while drawing more than 2597 BB. How would this have affected his projected cumulative totals?

Also, this model could be enhanced by considering such entities as the hit-by-pitch (HBP) statistic, on-base-average (OBA) and both stolen bases (SB) and caught stealing (CS). In this way, more offensive categories would be included.

What about pitching? We mentioned legendary Dodger southpaw Sandy Koufax. Koufax recorded 2396 strikeouts (K) in 2324.3 innings pitched (IP) during his shortened career. What if, for the sake of argument, we assume that he had pitched *an additional 800* innings? Can we use the EC approach with respect to pitching? Yes, we can.

To find Koufax's strikeout EC, we basically duplicate the procedure we used with the projected career cumulative hitting records of Ruth and Williams, since strikeouts are also a cumulative statistic. That is, we replace AB by K and substitute IP for PA. So if x is the number of additional K, and we assume an extra 800 IP, then

$$\frac{2396}{2324.3} = \frac{2396 + x}{2324.3 + 800}$$

yielding $x = 825$ additional K, when we solve for x. So the predicted prorated career strikeout total for Koufax would be $2396 + 825 = 3221$.

Now, let us further assume that Koufax would have been a 6 percent better pitcher during these additional 800 innings. Our kicker, k, is therefore 1.06. Hence, our new additional strikeout total becomes $(1.06)825 = 875$, giving a projected career total of $2396 + 875 = 3271$ We note that we could have arrived at this figure by using the formula

$$EC = 1 + \frac{Additional\ IP}{IP}(k) = 1 + \frac{800}{2324.3}(1.06) = 1.365$$

and computing $(1.365)(2396) = 3271$.

We summarize the technique of computing the EC for K in Figure 5.2.

How to Compute the Equivalence Coefficient (EC)
for Strikeouts (K)

- Determine the projected or desired number of new IP.

- Form the following proportion: $\dfrac{K}{IP} = \dfrac{K + y}{New\ IP}$

- Solve for y; this will give the additional number of K.

- $EC = 1 + \dfrac{Additional\ IP}{IP}(k)$, where k is the kicker. Note that $k > 1$, if the pitcher is assumed to be better during the additional IP; $k < 1$, if the pitcher is assumed to be worse during the additional IP. Finally, if $k = 1$, we are essentially prorating his statistics based on past performances.

- Multiply the EC by the desired cumulative statistic to get a projected total. This applies to Wins (W), Earned Runs (ER), etc.

- Note that the EC is *not* applied to relative statistics in the same way. See Earned Run Average (ERA) on the following pages.

Figure 5.2 Computing the equivalence coefficient for strikeouts

This technique can be used for all cumulative pitching statistics such as shutouts, decisions, etc. However, the approach must be modified when considering such statistics as earned run average.

A former sabermetrics student at Seton Hall University, Patrick Forgione, derived the following EC approach for projecting pitchers' ERA:

$$ERA = (9)\frac{ER+x}{IP+ky}$$

where ER are the number of earned runs allowed and x is the additional number of ER allowed; IP is the number of innings pitched and y is the additional number of IP; k is the kicker, where, as before, $k > 1$, if the pitcher is "better" and $k < 1$, if the pitcher is "worse."

To illustrate this, we consider the case of Dizzy Dean referenced at the beginning of this chapter. We first must determine reasonable values of x and y which should be based on his record. One way to approach this is to make certain assumptions, much like we did in the Ruth-Williams discussion above. Let's give Dean an additional 1000 IP; since Dean yielded 661 ER in 1963.66 IP, he averaged 0.337 ER / IP. If we simply prorate these numbers, then Dean would have given up a total of 337 ER in the additional 1000 IP (just multiply .337 by 1000). This preserves his lifetime ERA of 3.02.

But what if we assume that he would have been 5 percent better during these additional innings? This means that the "kicker" k has a value of 1.05. We now multiply the 1000 IP by 1.05. Using the formula above to project Dean's ERA, we have

$$ERA = (9)\frac{661+337}{1963.7+(1.05)(1000)} = 2.98$$

as his projected ERA.

As in the case of hitting, this instrument can be tweaked in many ways, and, as is in the case of all modeling, care must be exercised regarding any sort of prediction or projection.

A subtle mathematical observation should be made here regarding the EC approach pertaining to statistics like ERA. Because ERA is an average, rather than a cumulative statistic, and because there are two terms in both the numerator and the denominator, the coefficient for this statistic is nothing more than the kicker, which appears in the denominator of the formula.

We summarize the technique of using the EC approach for ERA in Table 5.3 on page 38.

THE EQUIVALENCE COEFFICIENT (EC) APPROACH FOR ERA

- Divide the original number of ER by the original number of IP, to get the ER per inning.

- Determine the additional number of IP. Call this number *y*.

- Multiply the additional number of IP by the ER per inning. Call this number *x*.

- Determine the kicker, *k*. As in the EC approach for hitting, we note that *k* > 1, if the pitcher is assumed to be better during the additional IP; *k* < 1, if the pitcher is assumed to be worse during the additional IP. If *k* = 1, then we are *prorating* his ERA.

- Use the formula $ERA = (9)\dfrac{ER + x}{IP + ky}$ to project this statistic.

Table 5.3 **Computing the equivalence coefficient for earned run average**

We end this chapter with a few words about what has been called the "unmeasurable" aspect of baseball: fielding. By its very nature, fielding is more subjective than hitting and pitching. (For instance, when is a catch "great"?) And, as was mentioned above, there are relatively few fielding measures discussed in baseball. Traditionally, assists (A), putouts (PO) and errors (E) have been the three most important components in virtually all fielding metrics — with Passed Balls (PB) included for catchers.

This being said, for cumulative statistics, such as career A or PO, the EC may be used, in virtually the same way we applied it in our discussions above pertaining to Ruth, Williams and Koufax.

For relative measures such as Fielding Average (FA) which is given by

$$FA = \frac{PO + A}{PO + A + E}$$

and Range Factor (RF) which is defined as

$$RF = \frac{PO + A}{G}$$

where *G* is the number of games played, the use of the EC concept would be applied in a similar way to that of Dizzy Dean ERA projection above. We will revisit the concept of the EC in subsequent chapters (for example, see Inning 9: Creating Measures and Doing Sabermetrics — Some Examples).

Easy Tosses

1. In his career, Hank Greenberg hit 331 HR in 5193 AB. He also walked 852 times, giving him a PA total of 6045. If Greenberg had 11,000 PA, and if we assume that he would have been 2 percent better for the additional PA, find his EC and project his career HR total.

2. Don Mattingly batted .307 over a 14-year career in which he had 7003 AB while drawing 588 BB. If we assume 12,000 PA, with Mattingly 1 percent better for the additional PA, project his career hit total.

3. Sandy Koufax pitched 2324.3 innings and gave up 713 earned runs. Project his ERA given an additional 1200 IP, assuming that he would have been 4 percent better during the additional IP.

4. J. R. Richards, a first-round draft pick by the Houston Astros, was one of the most feared pitchers of his era in the National League. In his shortened career, he pitched 1606 innings and allowed 562 earned runs. Project his ERA and strikeouts given an additional 1000 innings pitched, assuming he would have been 5 percent better.

Hard Sliders

1. Consider the following "split" statistics for Ted Williams:

Years	AB	W	H	HR
1939–1951	5086	1327	1763	323
1952–1960	2620	694	891	198

Give Williams an additional 1500 PA during the years 1939–1951 and assume that he was 8 percent better for the additional PA; furthermore, give him an additional 1000 PA for the remainder of his career while assuming that he was 3 percent better. Project his career totals for H, HR and BA.

2. Warren Spahn is considered to be one of the greatest left-handed starting pitchers of all time. He missed three years of playing ball from 1943 through 1945, due to his military service during World War II. Despite that, he still managed to win more games (363) than any other left-handed starting pitcher. Project his win total, given an additional 750 innings pitched, assuming he would have been 5 percent worse (it was the beginning of his career).

Inning 4: The Linear Weights School — Offense

Since the mid–1980s, there has been an explosion of new statistics, many commonly accepted by fans, players, writers, and official scorekeepers. Pete Palmer and John Thorn developed a statistic based on a formula known as "linear weights," in order to view the numbers of the game "as a means of encapsulating and comprehending experience." They went on to note that the tendency to scrutinize statistics is truly at the heart of baseball's hidden game. They recognized that there is an essential relationship between scoring runs and winning games. When the linear-weights model was developed, that relationship was analyzed using raw data in major league baseball's official records.

As a precursor to Thorn and Palmer's Linear Weights statistic, we must mention the works of F. C. Lane and George Lindsey. Ferdinand Cole Lane was a biologist who spent 27 years working for *Baseball Magazine* (he was editor from 1912 to 1937), analyzing baseball through statistics that were decades ahead of their time. Well before 1920, Lane conducted a study of exactly 1000 base hits, which occurred in 62 major league games. His goal was to assign a value to each hit and then study the probability of each hit producing a run. He started with a single being one-quarter, a double being one half, etc., and then added a few adjustments for runners on base. After a lengthy study, he developed the run value of a particular hit:

$$Runs = (0.30 \times 1B) + (0.60 \times 2B) + (0.90 \times 3B) + (1.15 \times HR)$$

A single was worth 30 percent of a run, a double was worth 60 percent of a run, a triple was worth 90 percent of a run, and a home run was worth 115 percent of a run. Lane used his formula to compare various type of hitters: singles hitters versus sluggers, for example. According to his relationship, a double was twice as good as a single, and a triple was three times as good, but a home run was not four times as good as a single (remember, this was the Deadball Era). After several years of continuing this study, Lane changed his coefficients, refining his run production model to:

Runs = $(0.457 \times 1B) + (0.786 \times 2B) + (1.15 \times 3B) + (1.55 \times HR)$

It could have been the arrival of the Longball Era (the emergence of Babe Ruth and other sluggers) which forced the change. Lane also believed that walks contributed to runs, with a run value of 0.164, but this opinion was not shared by many of his contemporaries.

Lane's work stood alone and quiet for about forty years as a measure for run production. In 1963, George Lindsey published an article in *Operations Research* entitled, "An Investigation of Strategies in Baseball," in which he was assigned run values to various offensive events, if those events led to scoring runs. For the first half of the twentieth century, the measure of a batter's effectiveness most used was the batting average (AVG), which is simply the number of hits divided by the number of at-bats. Two other measures were also frequently employed, the slugging percentage (SLG) and runs batted in (RBI). The slugging percentage is the ratio of total bases to the number of official at-bats. For example, in 1911, Ty Cobb had 248 hits in 591 at-bats; his batting average was .420. His hits consisted of 169 singles, 47 doubles, 24 triples, and 8 home runs. This amounted to 367 total bases, which gave him a slugging percentage of .621. He also had 127 RBI. Lindsey, not satisfied with these three measures, conducted a study of the effectiveness of each hit in a game. In particular, Lindsey claimed that a player's RBI total represented exploits of others (a runner had to be on base, unless the batter hit a home run) in addition to those of the batter. His approach was to assess batting effectiveness based on three assumptions:

- The batter's ultimate purpose is to cause runs to be scored.
- Batting effectiveness should not be measured for individuals based on situations that faced the batter when he came to the plate (since his batting actions did not create those situations).
- The probability of a batter getting different hits (single, double, etc.) is independent of the situation on the bases.

Lindsey stated that the third assumption listed above was probably not true, but he did acknowledge the perception of clutch hitters "who are particularly successful in critical situations." He accumulated out-versus-on-base data from 373 major league games played mostly in 1959 and 1960, and determined a value of a hit toward scoring runs based on the 24 different number-of-outs versus occupation-of-the-bases scenarios (no runners on with no outs, runner on first with no outs, bases loaded with two outs, etc.).

He used the out-base situation and converted the value of a hit into scoring a run. For example, in computing the value of a double, he found that a batter came to the plate with two outs and runners on first and second in 896 / 27027 = 0.033 appearances, or just over 3 percent of the time. The expected score was 0.403. After the double, the occasion awaiting the next hitter was either two outs and runner on third or two outs and runners at second and third. Lindsey weighted them both equally, and he determined a new expected score of 1.992. He claimed that the value of the double was 1.589 in this scenario, but to obtain the run value for an average situation, he added 0.033 × 1.589 to the terms in the other 23 number-of-outs versus occupation-of-the-bases scenarios. The resulting sum was 0.817, or 0.82 after rounding to two decimal places. He calculated the coefficients for the other hits in a similar fashion. Lindsey's formula for runs is:

$$\text{Runs} = (0.41 \times 1B) + (0.82 \times 2B) + (1.06 \times 3B) + (1.42 \times HR)$$

Notice that the coefficient for each type of hit is greater if more bases are reached. He explained that a home run increases the expected score, on average, by 1.42 runs. Specifically, a double was worth 1.97 as much as a single, a triple was worth 2.56 times as much as a single, and a home run was worth 3.42 times as much. This would indicate that the current weighting of 1:2:3:4 for slugging percentage overvalues the triple and home run. The key to Lindsey's research was recognizing that, in calculating the value of a run, a considerable factor was that a player did not make an out. By getting a hit, or, more importantly, not making an out, one batter allowed another batter to get to the plate. To use Lindsey's formula of batting effectiveness on Ty Cobb, we compute Cobb's value in runs for the 1911 season:

$$\text{Cobb's Runs} = (0.41 \times 169) + (0.82 \times 47) + (1.06 \times 24) + (1.42 \times 8) = 144.63$$

This means that Ty Cobb produced 144 more runs than the average batter. Wow! Using Lane's updated model (named the Lane 2), Cobb produced 154 more runs. We could re-compute the slugging percentage with Lindsey's coefficients as follows:

$$\text{SLG} = \frac{(1 \times 1B) + (1.97 \times 2B) + (2.56 \times 3B) + (3.42 \times HR)}{AB}$$

Lindsey calculated that an average batter has a one-in-three chance of reaching base, thereby allowing another batter to step up to the plate with the same chance to reach base. In his own words, the "allowance for deviation from average performance of the batter at the plate ... can be made by a shrewd manager who knows his players." This was ground-breaking research into modeling and predicting the runs produced by a hitter, despite Lindsey's omission of other offensive events, such as walks, steals, caught stealing, sacrifices, etc.

Other researchers have subsequently tried to capture the essence of runs and wins. Steve Mann created the run productivity average (RPA), but it placed too much emphasis on runs batted in (RBI). Mann assigned values based on a study of 12,000 plate appearances. His formula was:

$$RPA = \frac{(0.51 \times 1B) + (0.82 \times 2B) + (1.38 \times 3B) + (2.63 \times HR) + (0.25 \times BB) + (0.15 \times SB) - (0.25 \times CS)}{\text{Plate Appearances}} + 0.016$$

This formula was developed with values concerned with the number of runs and RBIs that each offensive event produced. The drawback in this is that an RBI is credited to the batter who drives in the run and it doesn't matter how the runner who scored came around the bases to do so. John Thorn and Pete Palmer posed the following scenario to consider: Suppose the leadoff hitter in an inning reaches on an error. The next batter doubles, allowing the runner on first to advance to third base. The third batter of the inning grounds out to an infielder, whose only play is at first base. The batter, who just made an out, is credited with a run batted in. The runner who reached on an error is credited with a run. The second batter who reached via an actual hit (in fact, the only batter to hit safely) is given no credit at all.

In 1978, in an effort to understand the value of a run produced, Pete Palmer developed a computer simulation, taking into account all major league games played since 1901. His goal was to equate measured quantities to actual statistics from league play and model run production. His simulation provided run values of each event in terms of net runs produced above the average amount. If an event was unmeasured, such as the probability of a player advancing an extra base (say, going from first to third on a single, instead of just advancing to second), then Palmer assigned a value to that probability. These additionally assigned values were based on Palmer's in-depth play-by-play analysis of over one hundred World Series games. These values then had significance related to individual accomplishments. Additionally, his simulation could then compare an individual player's performance to an average player's performance for a given season. Palmer then went one step further and compared his run values of the different offensive events by twenty-year eras. Expressing his run values in "beyond-average runs," which means how well did a player produce a run above the league average, he found that the values were remarkably similar from one era to the next. Listed in Table 6.1 is his chart of how various events produced run values.

Event	1901–20	1921–40	1941–60	1961–77
Home Run	1.36	1.40	1.42	1.42
Triple	1.02	1.05	1.03	1.00
Double	0.82	0.83	0.80	0.77
Single	0.46	0.50	0.47	0.45
Walk/HBP	0.32	0.35	0.35	0.33
Stolen Base	0.20	0.22	0.19	0.19
Caught Stealing	−0.33	−0.39	−0.36	−0.32
Out*	−0.24	−0.30	−0.27	−0.25

Table 6.1 Palmer's run values of various events, by periods

In his chart, Palmer noted that "an out is considered to be a hitless at-bat and its value set so that the sum of all events times their frequency is zero, thus establishing zero as the base line, or norm, for performance." A few years after Palmer published his study, statistician Dave Smith (of *Retrosheet*) suggested to Palmer that he might adjust the coefficients for stolen base and caught stealing events, as they were situation dependent. In a 1980 article entitled, "Maury Wills and the Value of a Stolen Base," Smith wrote that players elected to steal bases, and stolen bases were attempted more frequently in close baseball games. Palmer accepted the advice and revised his coefficients to be 0.30 and −0.60, respectively.

John Thorn then teamed with Pete Palmer to develop the Linear Weights model for predicting runs produced by a batter. They published The Hidden Game of Baseball in 1984. Their new model took an in-depth view into scoring runs. Run values evolved as playing conditions changed, and the two authors also wrote that run values depend on the batting order and batting position. Traditional leadoff batters are not power hitters, so a home run is not worth as much to them as to a clean-up batter. The 1984 linear-weights formula for batting runs is

Batting Runs = $(0.46 \times 1B) + (0.80 \times 2B) + (1.02 \times 3B) + (1.40 \times HR) + [0.33 \times (BB + HBP)] + (0.30 \times SB) - (0.60 \times CS) - [0.25 \times (AB - H)] - (0.50 \times OOB)$

According to the linear-weights model, a home run is worth, on average, 1.40 runs over the course of an average season, while getting caught stealing loses a hitter 0.60 runs. The last term in this formula is an effort to take outs from plate appearances into account; subtracting hits and walks from plate appearances gives outs, and this term received a negative run weight. According to Thorn and Palmer, "while a single or walk always has a potential run value, a long fly does not unless a man happens to be posed at third base." When this formula was first revealed, statisticians expected to see events such as sacrifices, sacrifice hits, grounded into double plays, and reached on error. Notice also that the coefficients for 1B, 2B, 3B, and HR are very close to those proposed by both Lane's second model and Lindsey's model. Further, Thorn and Palmer postulated that a home run was only worth about three times as much as a single, which is close to a half run less than suggested by Lindsey's formula. In fact, they omit the stealing, caught stealing and outs-on-base terms when comparing the great players of the past, as data for caught stealing is not known. They thus used a condensed form for linear weights, given by:

Batting Runs = (0.47 × 1B) + (0.78 × 2B) + (1.09 × 3B) + (1.40 × HR) + [0.33 × (BB + HBP)] − [0.25 × (AB − H)]

Notice that the value of a single is 0.47 runs, and each extra-base hit (double, triple, home run) has a value of 0.31 times the number of bases beyond a single. They claim that this condensed version is accurate to within a fraction of a run.

How effective is the Linear Weights model? First, we mention that, just as with George Lindsey's run model, Thorn and Palmer's linear-weights model is a deviation from average performance. A batter with a positive linear-weights run production is above the average player, while a batter with a negative run production would be below average. Let's consider a comparison of selected players from the 1960s. Table 6.2 shows a listing of all of the players (non-pitchers) who won the Most Valuable Player Award from 1960 through 1969 in both the National and American Leagues. In the columns next to their names are the seasons in which each won the league MVP award. We then list the seasonal offensive data and the linear-weights-model run production (LW Runs, using the condensed formula).

Player	Year	H	1B	2B	3B	HR	BB	HBP	SB	CS	AB	LW RUNS
NATIONAL LEAGUE												
Dick Groat	1960	186	154	26	4	2	39	4	0	2	573	17.26
Frank Robinson	1961	176	100	32	7	37	71	10	22	3	545	65.87
Maury Wills	1962	208	179	13	10	6	51	2	104	13	695	9.31
Ken Boyer	1964	185	121	30	10	24	70	2	3	5	628	37.78
Willie Mays	1965	177	101	21	3	52	76	0	9	4	558	69.75
Roberto Clemente	1966	202	131	31	11	29	46	0	7	5	638	44.52
Orlando Cepeda	1967	183	121	37	0	25	62	12	11	2	563	50.15
Willie McCovey	1969	157	84	26	2	45	121	4	0	0	491	82.69

Player	Year	H	1B	2B	3B	HR	BB	HBP	SB	CS	AB	LW RUNS
(continued)												
AMERICAN LEAGUE												
Roger Maris	1960	141	77	18	7	39	70	3	2	2	499	47.05
Roger Maris	1961	159	78	16	4	61	94	7	0	0	590	64.48
Mickey Mantle	1962	121	75	15	1	30	122	1	9	0	377	66.63
Elston Howard	1963	140	85	21	6	28	35	6	0	0	487	28.85
Brooks Robinson	1964	194	128	35	3	28	51	4	1	0	612	43.58
Zoilo Versalles	1965	182	106	45	12	19	41	7	27	5	666	19.44
Frank Robinson	1966	182	97	34	2	49	87	10	8	5	576	76.40
Carl Yastrzemski	1967	189	110	31	4	44	91	4	10	8	579	75.69
Harmon Killebrew	1969	153	82	20	2	49	145	5	8	2	555	73.92

Table 6.2 Linear weights batting runs for MVPs from 1960 to 1969

From Table 6.2, we notice that Willie McCovey's 1969 MVP season with the San Francisco Giants led to a batting run production of 82.69 runs above average. Dick Groat, on the other hand, won the 1960 Most Valuable Player Award with a run production of only 17.26 runs. When Maury Wills' 104 stolen bases are taken away, his run production fell to 9.31 total batting runs. All of the batters listed were "above average," but some were notably more than others. Despite only 377 official at-bats in 1962, the American League's MVP, Mickey Mantle, still produced 66 more runs than the average player, according to the linear-weights model. Compare his production to his 1962 National League counterpart, Maury Wills. Wills had over 300 more at-bats, 87 more hits, and 95 more stolen bases, yet his run production is a fraction of Mantle's.

Let's compare the 1962 seasons of Mantle and Wills using more traditional statistics. Mantle's batting average in 1962 was 0.321; his on-base percentage was 0.486, and his slugging percentage was a respectable 0.605. He had 228 total bases. Wills, in comparison, had a 0.299 batting average, 0.347 on-base percentage, and 0.373 slugging percentage, accounting for 259 total bases. Wills' stolen bases accounted for 77 percent of his run production. Mantle's nine stolen bases accounted for about 4 percent of his total runs. However, Mantle's 30 home runs and 123 walks and HBP dwarf Wills' six home runs and 53 walks and HBP. Without the stolen bases, Wills does not appear to have contributed many runs above the average.

In 1984, Thorn and Palmer mentioned that their linear-weights statistics have a "shadow stat which tracks its accuracy to a remarkable degree and is a breeze to calculate: OPS, or On Base Average Plus Slugging Percentage." They went on to mention that the correlation between linear weights and OPS over the course of an average team's regular season was 99.7 percent. OPS has since become a fixture in measuring the offensive production of a player. The linear-weights model is just as insightful. In 1962, Mantle's OPS was 0.321 + 0.605 = 0.926. Wills, by comparison, had an OPS of 0.299 + 0.373 = 0.672, or 0.254 points lower. High OPS correlates to producing more runs above average for a batter's team. However, since OPS is not expressed in terms of runs, Thorn and Palmer felt that it was a less versatile statistic than their linear-weights. They explained that run scoring for teams is proportional to the on-base average times the slugging percentage (also known as the SLOB), while runs produced by a batter in an average lineup are proportional to his on-base average plus slugging percentage (OPS).

The linear weights batting run-production model seeks to assign run values to each offensive play. Certain events are not accounted for, however. As mentioned earlier, it does not predict runs based on sacrifices, sacrifice flies, grounded into double plays, or plays in which the batter reached on an error.

Pete Palmer published another article in the inaugural issue (1982) of *The National Pastime: A Review of Baseball History.* Palmer was chairman of SABR's statistical analysis committee and John Thorn was the editor of *The National Pastime.* In an article entitled, "Runs and Wins," Palmer expanded on a notion which he felt had received little attention to that point: the relationship of runs scored and allowed to wins and losses. He was interested in "how many games a team ought to have won, how many it did win, and which teams' actual won-lost records varied far from their probable won-lost records." In this article, Palmer cites earlier work by Earnshaw Cook. In 1964, Cook published *Percentage Baseball,* which examined major league results from 1950 through 1960. In that paper, Cook determined that the winning percentage of a team was given by the following formula:

$$\text{Winning Percentage} = 0.484 \times \frac{\text{Runs Scored}}{\text{Runs Allowed}}$$

The example provided in the paper cites the 1965 Minnesota Twins, who scored 774 runs while yielding 600. Their winning percentage should have been 0.484 times 774 divided by 600, or 0.630. The '65 Twins, in fact, finished the season with 102 wins and 60 losses, for a winning percentage of 0.623. In "Runs and Wins," Palmer states that his work showed that, "as a rough rule of thumb, each additional ten runs scored (or ten less runs allowed) produced one extra win." He also found that high-scoring teams needed more runs to produce a win. Interestingly, he determined the exact run-per-win factor for an individual team to be equal to ten times the square root of the actual number of runs scored per inning by both teams. So, if two average teams both score 4.5 runs in a game, that is one total run per inning. Taking the square root of one and multiplying by ten yields a run-per-win factor of ten. This means that, using Lindsey's model, Ty Cobb would have personally contributed over 14 wins to his 1911 Tigers team. Using linear weights, Cobb produced 107.33 runs (caught stealing statistics are not available for that season), which converts to about 11 wins, still a very impressive total.

Let's revisit the Most Valuable Players from the 1960s. Using Palmer's run-per-win factor of ten, we see that Willie McCovey contributed more than 8 wins above average (WAA) for his Giants squad, while teammate Willie Mays contributed seven WAA for his 1965 Giants team. Frank Robinson had seven WAA for each of his teams, the 1961 Reds and the 1966 Orioles; Carl Yastrzemski produced seven WAA for the 1967 Red Sox, and Harmon Killebrew has 7.5 WAA for his 1969 Twins. It's interesting that Dick Groat won the 1960 Most Valuable Player Award in the National League by contributing only about one and a half WAA to the Pirates. Groat won the MVP by a landslide vote, garnering 16 of 22 first-place votes. However, his Pittsburgh teammates were well represented in the balloting; Don Hoak finished second, Cy Young Award winner Vern Law finished tied for sixth, Roberto Clemente finished eighth, Roy Face finished twelfth, and Smoky Burgess finished tied for twentieth (see the "Easy Tosses" at the end of the chapter to determine the linear weights runs for Groat's teammates in 1960).

The Thorn and Palmer linear-weights model has been revised a few times since it was first published in the eighties, taking into account changes in the situational values. The coefficients for the values of the various hits (single, doubles, etc.) have been modified to account for actual changes in run production. In the 2006 edition of *Baseball Encyclopedia*, the formula is listed as:

$$\text{Batting Runs} = (0.47 \times 1B) + (0.38 \times 2B) + (0.55 \times 3B) + (0.93 \times HR) + [0.33 \times (BB + HBP)] - [ABF \times (AB - H)]$$

The "ABF" term is a league batting factor term, which scales the value of the average batter to 0. ABF is computed according to the following calculation:

$$\text{ABF} = \frac{(0.47 \times 1B) + (0.38 \times 2B) + (0.55 \times 3B) + (0.93 \times HR) + [0.33 \times (BB + HBP)]}{AB - (LGF \times H)}$$

All of the statistics in the ABF equation are league statistics. In addition, the "LGF" term is known as the league factor, and it adjusts for the quality of league play. It is scaled to 1 for American League and National

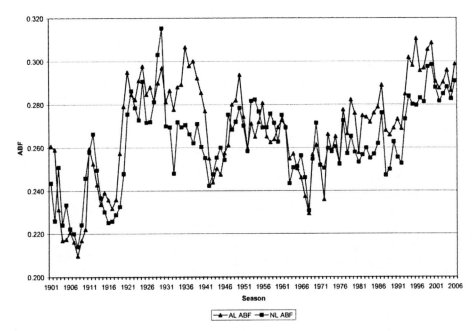

Figure 6.1 ABF for American and National Leagues, 1901 to 2006

League play, and it equals 0.8 for Union Association play (1884) and 0.9 for Federal League play (1914–1915).

This new batting runs formula thus becomes very involved. Why? Because the league batting-term factor, ABF, will vary from season to season and from American League to National League. For example, in 1966, the American League batting-term factor was 0.246, whereas forty years later in 2006 it was 0.299. Figure 6.1 shows how the ABF has changed since 1901. In addition, the new formula accounts only for batting runs and not for any runs produced by stealing bases. The coefficients for hits have changed from the 1984 formula.

From Figure 6.1, notice the relatively low ABF values during the Dead-ball Era and then the significant spike in values at the beginning of the 1920s. Interestingly, since the beginning of the designated hitter (1975), the ABF for the American League has been consistently higher than that of the National League. This should be expected, as the pitchers' lower batting statistics are included in the NL ABF. Further, the steady increase in the annual value of the ABF correlates to a lower overall run production for hitters (a higher coefficient multiplies the at-bat minus hits total, thereby lowering the Linear Weights batting-runs value). The more recent years' ABF for both American and National Leagues are listed in Figure 6.2.

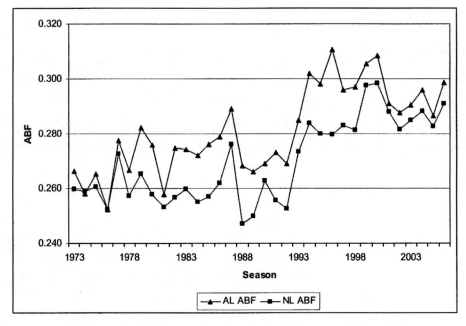

Figure 6.2 ABF for American and National Leagues, 1973 to 2006

Who is the best player of all time according to linear weights? In *The Hidden Game of Baseball*, Babe Ruth, not surprisingly, was listed as the hands-down leader in both career and single-season batting runs (Thorn and Palmer calculated their lists through the 1983 seasons). How have batters fared recently, during the so-called Longball Era? Using the 2006 Linear Weights formula with the ABF, let's compare some of the great hitters using some of their premier seasons: Ty Cobb in 1911, Babe Ruth in 1921, Rogers Hornsby in 1925, Lou Gehrig in 1927, Ted Williams in 1941, Stan Musial in 1948, Mickey Mantle in 1957, Frank Robinson in 1966, Rod Carew in 1977, George Brett in 1980, Barry Bonds in 2001, Ichiro Suzuki in 2004, and Albert Pujols in 2005. Their statistics are listed in Table 6.3.

Player	Year	AVG	H	1B	2B	3B	HR	BB	HBP	AB	LW RUNS
Ty Cobb	1911	0.420	248	169	47	24	8	44	8	591	46.08
Babe Ruth	1921	0.378	204	85	44	16	59	145	4	540	70.40
Rogers Hornsby	1924	0.424	227	145	43	14	25	89	2	536	61.18
Lou Gehrig	1927	0.373	218	101	52	18	47	109	3	584	52.38
Ted Williams	1941	0.406	185	112	33	3	37	147	3	456	75.68
Stan Musial	1948	0.376	230	127	46	18	39	79	3	611	48.13

Player	Year	AVG	H	1B	2B	3B	HR	BB	HBP	AB	LW RUNS
Mickey Mantle	1957	0.365	173	105	28	6	34	146	0	474	63.27
Frank Robinson	1966	0.316	182	97	34	2	49	87	10	576	40.26
Rod Carew	1977	0.388	239	171	38	16	14	69	3	616	35.73
George Brett	1980	0.390	175	109	33	9	24	58	1	449	34.90
Barry Bonds	2001	0.328	156	49	32	2	73	177	9	476	73.42
Barry Bonds	2002	0.370	149	70	31	2	46	198	9	403	85.33
Albert Pujols	2003	0.359	212	117	51	1	43	79	10	591	36.29
Ichiro Suzuki	2004	0.372	262	225	24	5	8	49	4	704	11.77

Table 6.3 Linear weights batting runs for selected hitters

From this exercise, we see that Barry Bonds' 2002 season leads the way as the best season, even better than his record home run year of 2001. Although Ichiro Suzuki established the new record for hits in 2004, his run production was low, due to his lack of extra base hits and walks (he was penalized for his large number of at-bats and the corresponding 442 outs). The best season listed in Thorn and Palmer's book was Ruth's 1921 season. With the new formula, Ruth falls below Ted Williams, as well as below Bonds. Is the formula missing something? A degree of relativity is being introduced. Higher OPS and much larger batting averages lead to more runs per game.

When the linear-weights concept was first introduced, it was a refreshing yet powerful tool which could be used to compare a player's performance with other players. The shadow statistic, on-base plus slugging (OPS), which was mentioned earlier, has been a benchmark in recent years. Most studies begin with an analysis of a player's OPS and go from there. We have seen that the correlation between OPS and linear weights is 99.7 percent over an average team's regular season.

How does OPS correlate with the accolades that are handed out to star players at the end of the season? Many player's contracts now include incentive clauses to financially reward them if they are elected to the All-Star Game, or if they win a batting title, or for a host of other awards. (As an aside, in Japan, there is a daily incentive, which is separate from a player's salary, and it is known as *kantoku shou*, which, translated literally, means manager prize. The Japanese manager gives money to a player who plays particularly well in a game — instant cash.) The Most Valuable Player Award is bestowed by the Baseball Writers Association of America (BBWAA) on the player who is deemed the best player in his league for the entire season. Since 1944, the MVP Award has been called the Kenesaw Mountain Landis Award in honor of the game's first commissioner; the annual winners receive a trophy, and their names are engraved on a plaque in the National Baseball Library at the National Baseball Hall of Fame and Museum in Cooperstown, New York. Since 1938, votes have been cast using the *ranked choice* method. In this system, each voting member of the BBWAA votes for up to ten players, ranking each player from 1 to 10. The player ranked first on a ballot is then assigned 14 points, the player ranked second is assigned 9 points, on down to the player ranked who is ranked 10th, who receives one point.

It is interesting to examine the statistics of the winner of the Kenesaw Mountain Landis Award. How often does the league's Most Valuable Player lead the American or National League in OPS or linear-weights runs? In Table 6.4, we present the statistics for the top three Kenesaw Mountain Landis Award vote-getters in both the American and National Leagues, for the years 2002 through 2006 (listed in order of votes received). What conclusions can we draw from this table?

Year	American League MVP	OPS	National League MVP	OPS
2003	1. Alex Rodriguez	0.996	1. Barry Bonds	1.278
	2. Carlos Delgado	1.019	2. Albert Pujols	1.106
	3. Jorge Posada	0.923	3. Gary Sheffield	1.023
2004	1. Vladimir Guerrero	0.989	1. Barry Bonds	1.421
	2. Gary Sheffield	0.927	2. Adrian Beltre	1.017
	3. Manny Ramirez	1.010	3. Albert Pujols	1.072
2005	1. Alex Rodriguez	1.031	1. Albert Pujols	1.039
	2. David Ortiz	1.001	2. Andruw Jones	0.922
	3. Vladimir Guerrero	0.959	3. Derrek Lee	1.080
2006	1. Justin Morneau	0.934	1. Ryan Howard	1.084
	2. Derek Jeter	0.900	2. Albert Pujols	1.102
	3. David Ortiz	1.049	3. Lance Berkman	1.041

Table 6.4 Comparing league MVP ranking with OPS

Here are some more details: in 2006, Travis Hafner led the American League vote-getters in OPS (with 1.098), yet he finished 8th in the end-of-season MVP voting. In 2004, Manny Ramirez was the only American League MVP vote-getter whose OPS was greater than 1.000, yet he finished third when the votes were tallied. In 2003, Manny Ramirez again had an OPS above 1.000 (1.014), and his batting average was 27 points higher than Alex Rodriguez's, but Ramirez finished 6th in the voting. In the National League in 2003, Albert Pujols had a batting average of .359 (compared to Barry Bonds' .341), 212 hits (to Bonds' 133), in over 200 more at-bats than Bonds.

Yet Bonds won the award overwhelmingly. So what? This comparison shows that while statistics often support an argument for end-of-season tributes, non-sabermetrical arguments also play a part. Did Bonds win the 2003 award because he had already won the previous two years and five overall (the 2004 award gave him a record seven)?

Easy Tosses

1. Using George Lindsey's ratios of hit values, calculate the slugging percentage of the following players in the specific season:

Player	Season	AB	H	2B	3B	HR
Ty Cobb	1911	591	248	47	24	8
Lou Gehrig	1931	619	211	31	15	46
Babe Ruth	1921	540	204	44	16	59
Ted Williams	1941	456	185	33	3	37

2. In 1983, Baltimore Orioles shortstop Cal Ripken won the American League Most Valuable Player Award over his teammate, first baseman Eddie Murray, in a close contest. Based on the original linear weights batting run production, who should have won the award? Here is the data:

Player	AB	H	2B	3B	HR	BB	HBP	SB	CS
Cal Ripken	663	211	47	2	27	58	0	0	4
Eddie Murray	582	178	30	3	33	86	3	5	1

3. Using the original linear-weights model, calculate the batting runs for the starting line-up of the 1960 Pittsburgh Pirates: C Smoky Burgess, 1B Dick Stuart, 2B Bill Mazeroski, SS Dick Groat, 3B Don Hoak, and Outfielders Roberto Clemente, Bob Skinner, and Bill Virdon. Here is the data:

Player	AB	H	2B	3B	HR	BB	HBP	SB	CS
Smoky Burgess	337	99	15	2	7	35	0	0	1
Dick Stuart	438	114	17	5	23	39	0	0	0
Bill Mazeroski	538	147	21	5	11	40	1	4	0
Don Hoak	553	156	24	9	16	74	1	3	2
Dick Groat	573	186	26	4	2	39	4	0	2
Roberto Clemente	570	179	22	6	16	39	2	4	5
Bob Skinner	571	156	33	6	15	59	1	11	8
Bill Virdon	409	108	16	9	8	40	0	8	2

4. Listed below are the Kenesaw Mountain Landis Award winners for the American League Most Valuable Player for the years 1995 through 2002. Surprisingly, none of the league MVPs were on the World Champion team the year they won. Using a reference (i.e., statistics on the Internet), determine each player's OPS. Who led the league in OPS each year and who on the World Series champion team had the highest OPS?

Year	American League MVP
1995	Mo Vaughn
1996	Juan Gonzalez
1997	Ken Griffey, Jr.
1998	Juan Gonzalez
1999	Ivan Rodriguez
2000	Jason Giambi
2001	Ichiro Suzuki
2002	Miguel Tejada

Hard Sliders

1. Calculate the batting runs for the top five home run hitters of all time, for the season in which each won his first Most Valuable Player Award: Hank Aaron in 1957, Barry Bonds in 1991, Babe Ruth in 1923, Willie Mays in 1954, and Sammy Sosa in 1998. Who contributed the most wins to his own team? Here is the data:

Player	Year	AB	H	2B	3B	HR	BB	HBP	SB	CS
Aaron	1957	615	198	27	6	44	57	0	1	1
Bonds	1990	519	156	32	3	33	93	3	52	13
Mays	1954	565	195	33	13	41	66	12	8	5
Ruth	1923	522	205	45	13	41	170	4	17	21
Sosa	1998	643	198	20	0	66	73	1	18	9

2. Consider the following Hall of Fame catchers, all of whom played before 1930: Roger Bresnahan, Buck Ewing, and Ray Schalk. Who contributed the most runs to his own team (use the condensed form for Linear Weights Batting Runs)? Here is the data:

Player	AB	H	2B	3B	HR	1B	BB	HBP
Roger Bresnahan	4481	1252	218	71	26	937	714	67
Buck Ewing	5363	1625	250	178	72	1125	392	9
Ray Shalk	5306	1345	199	49	11	1086	638	59

3. Only six players have hit 60 or more doubles in a season (notice in which era they all occurred). They are:

Player	Team	Year	Doubles
Earl Webb	Boston (AL)	1931	67
George Burns	Cleveland (AL)	1926	64
Joe Medwick	St. Louis (NL)	1936	64
Hank Greenberg	Detroit (AL)	1934	63
Paul Waner	Pittsburgh (NL)	1932	62
Charlie Gehringer	Detroit (AL)	1936	60

Which of these hitters contributed the most linear-weights runs (condensed form) to his team during the indicated season?

Inning 5:
The Linear Weights School —
Pitching and Defense

Hall of Fame manager Earl Weaver said that the key to winning baseball games is pitching, fundamentals, and three-run homers. In chapter 4 we discussed the Linear Weights formula for batting runs which predicts the number of runs produced by an average baseball team based on all of the offensive events recorded during the game. It is used to evaluate a batter's performance. Given that Thorn and Palmer viewed a home run as being worth three times as much as a single, Weaver's three-run homer would indeed be effective. What about defense and pitching? In this chapter we summarize the linear-weights models for fielding and pitching, beginning with the latter.

Pitching Runs

In *Total Baseball*, Thorn and Palmer wrote that "determining the run contributions of pitchers is much easier than determining those of fielders or batters, though not quite so simple as that of base stealers. Actual runs allowed are known, as are innings pitched." Roger Clemens has had a Hall of Fame career. At the close of the 2007 season, the Rocket had won 354 games, for a winning percentage of .658. His seven Cy Young Awards as his league's top pitcher are a record. He has struck out 4672 opposing batters, which is second all-time, and his 24-year career earned run average (3.12) is almost one and a half runs below the league average over that same stretch. Seven times he led his league in earned run average. Both fans and opposing batters viewed the eleven-time All-Star Clemens as a dominant force every time he took the mound. Our questions is: how much did his performance contribute to his teams' successes? Can we determine the run contributions of his starts? Should he have won seven Cy Young Awards?

The linear-weights pitching-runs model assumes that pitchers are responsible only for earned runs. Thorn and Palmer argue that the earned run average statistic is an indication of a pitcher's rate of efficiency, not an indication of his actual benefit to a team's overall performance. As an example, if a team has two pitchers with identical ERAs who are compared against a higher league ERA, and pitcher A pitched in twice as many innings as pitcher B, then pitcher A must be worth twice as much as pitcher B to his team. The linear-weights pitching-runs statistic seeks to measure the number of runs, beyond the average, that a pitcher has prevented from scoring. The formula for earned run average is:

$$\text{Earned Run Average (ERA)} = \frac{\text{Earned Runs} \times 9}{\text{Innings Pitched}}$$

What about the average number of runs for a pitcher? This will equate to a pitching runs number of zero. The average number of runs is:

$$\text{Average Runs} = \frac{\text{League ERA} \times \text{Innings Pitched}}{9}$$

For example, in 2002, Roger Clemens had an ERA of 4.35 in 180 innings pitched for the New York Yankees. The American League average ERA was 4.38 runs (almost identical). Had Clemens' ERA also been 4.38, he would have held opposing batters in check at the league average, regardless of the number of innings he pitched. In 2005, by contrast, Clemens, then with the Houston Astros, authored an amazing ERA of 1.87 in over 211 innings pitched. This was the lowest ERA for a season in Clemens' 23-year career. The National League average was 4.14 runs. Surely, Clemens saved a significant number of runs that an average pitche, pitching in his place, might have allowed. How to find that number? Thorn and Palmer's linear-weights pitching-runs formula is straightforward and simple:

$$\text{Pitching Runs} = \text{Innings Pitched} \times \frac{\text{League ERA}}{9} - \text{Earned Runs}$$

Notice that the last term in the formula is actual earned runs allowed, not the earned run average. Pitching runs provides a difference of earned runs allowed at a league average, for the given number of innings pitched, and actual earned run allowed. Let's calculate Clemens' pitching runs for 2005:

$$\text{Pitching Runs} = 211.3 \times \frac{4.14}{9} - 44 = 53.20$$

This shows that Roger Clemens was 53.2 runs better than the average National League pitcher in 2005. Using the accepted notion that ten runs equates to a win, Clemens would have turned an average 81–81 National League team into a team with a record of 86–76. (The Astros finished the 2005 regular season at 89–73). There is a second formula for pitching runs that rearranges terms:

$$\text{Pitching Runs} = \frac{\text{Innings Pitched} \times (\text{League ERA} - \text{Pitcher's ERA})}{9}$$

Substituting Clemens' 2005 numbers yields:

$$\text{Pitching Runs} = \frac{211.3 \times (4.14 - 1.87)}{9} = 53.29$$

This second formula, involving only innings pitched and earned run averages, is best employed when evaluating the performance of pitchers for whom the number of earned runs is not available, but the ERA is known. Notice the slight error in the two approaches; round-off error for the two ERAs can lead to a slight disagreement in pitching-run values.

In 2001, Roger Clemens won his unprecedented sixth Cy Young Award. The voting was not close. The New York Yankees' Clemens picked up 21 of 28 first-place votes, and his total number of points was twice as much as the next vote-getter, the Oakland Athletics' Mark Mulder. Did Roger win a sixth because he already had five? Was he the best pitcher in the American League, relative to other pitchers? Let's compare the six pitchers who received votes for the AL Cy Young Award in 2001. They are listed in the order of voting points finish in Table 7.1. The league ERA was 4.48.

Pitcher	Team	Points	W-L	IP	ERA
Roger Clemens	NYY	122	20–3	220	3.51
Mark Mulder	OAK	60	21–8	229	3.45
Freddy Garcia	SEA	55	18–6	239	3.05
Jamie Moyer	SEA	12	20–6	210	3.43
Mike Mussina	NYY	2	17–11	229	3.15
Tim Hudson	OAK	1	18–9	235	3.37

Table 7.1 Cy Young Award voting finish, 2001

At first glance, the earned run averages of the six pitchers are comparable, although Freddie Garcia had close to a half run smaller ERA than Clemens. Innings pitched are also similar. Clemens' won-lost record was astonishing (almost 87 percent), but Jamie Moyer also had a great season. Using the second pitching runs (PR) formula, we determine the following:

Pitcher	IP	ERA	PR	Team's W-L
Roger Clemens	220	3.51	23.71	95–65
Mark Mulder	229	3.45	26.21	102–60
Freddy Garcia	239	3.05	37.97	116–46
Jamie Moyer	210	3.43	24.50	116–46
Mike Mussina	229	3.15	33.84	95–65
Tim Hudson	235	3.37	28.98	102–60

Table 7.2 AL pitching runs, 2001

Of the six pitchers receiving votes, Clemens has the lowest pitching-runs value. That equates to the fewest wins afforded to his team. Did his won-lost record push him that far ahead of his rivals? Should he have received the Cy Young Award? Freddie Garcia earned over 14 more pitching runs, which equates to about one and a half more wins for his team. The Mariners sailed to a record 116 victories in 2001.

Let's inspect the data further. Compare Clemens with his teammate Mike Mussina, who had ten more pitching runs. Mussina pitched 8 more innings than Clemens, but he allowed six fewer earned runs. Not shown is the fact that Mussina had four complete games, including three shutouts, in 2001, while Clemens had none of each. Opponents batted .237 against Mussina while hitting .246 against Clemens. Clemens did receive a higher run support from the Yankees when he pitched, and Mussina did offer one more win for the Yankees from his pitching runs than did Clemens. The vote is in the history books, but sabermetricians can ponder the 2001 Cy Young Award vote using linear weights.

Thorn and Palmer incorporate efficiency and durability into their pitching-runs formula. If a pitcher is consistently better than average, his team will benefit more and his linear-weights pitching-runs value will be higher. For example, if a pitcher is allowing one less earned run per game than the average pitcher, his pitching-runs total will increase with more innings pitched. One problem emerges, however. If we look at *Baseball-reference. com*'s listing of the single-season leaders for innings pitched (IP), we will notice that the top 100 on that listing are all players who pitched before 1901. At the very top of the list is Will White, with 680 innings in 1879. Down at number 100 is Gus Weyhing at 469⅔ innings in 1892. The 1918 Chicago Cubs' Hippo Vaughn was the first pitcher to lead either league in innings pitched with a total under 300 innings (290⅓). The last pitcher to pitch over 300 innings in a season was Philadelphia's Steve Carlton, who had 304 innings pitched in 1980, the season the Phillies won their only World

Series. No pitcher since 1980 has pitched more than 300 innings in a season. What does this mean? A pre–1900 pitcher with a mediocre ratio of earned run average to the league earned run average will amass an enormous number of pitching runs due to the large number of innings pitched. Thorn and Palmer list the ten best pitchers with pitching linear weights since 1961 in Table 7.3.

Pitcher	Season	IP	ERA	Lg ERA	Pitch LWTS
Sandy Koufax	1966	323	1.73	3.28	55.72
Bob Gibson	1968	305	1.12	2.90	60.32
Ron Guidry	1978	274	1.74	3.63	57.54
Dean Chance	1964	279	1.65	3.30	51.15
Jim Palmer	1975	323	2.09	3.52	51.32
Wilbur Wood	1971	334	1.91	3.61	63.09
Vida Blue	1971	312	1.82	3.33	52.35
Steve Carlton	1972	347	1.97	3.59	62.46
Sandy Koufax	1965	336	2.04	3.26	45.55
Tom Seaver	1971	287	1.76	3.40	52.30

Table 7.3 Top ten in pitching runs, 1961–1984

Bob Gibson, Dean Chance, and Sandy Koufax are the only pitchers after 1916 to have more than ten shutouts in a single season. Those shutouts directly contributed to their low earned run averages, which in turn correlates to a high pitching runs value.

What about recent pitchers? Let's compare the Cy Young Award seasons of the five winners in the American League from 2005, 1995, 1985, 1975, and 1965.

	Year	Tm	W	L	GS	CG	SHO	IP	H	R	ER	ERA	LgERA
B. Colon	2005	LAA	21	8	33	2	0	222.7	215	93	86	3.48	4.19
R. Johnson	1995	SEA	18	2	30	6	3	214.3	159	65	59	2.48	4.86
B. Saberhagen	1985	KCR	20	6	32	10	1	235.3	211	79	75	2.87	4.15
J. Palmer	1975	BAL	23	11	38	25	10	323.0	253	87	75	2.09	3.52

Table 7.4 Comparison of Cy Young Award winners

At first glance, Randy Johnson's 1995 season stands out as one in which his personal ERA was almost half of the league ERA. His winning percentage was phenomenal. However, one-third of his starts resulted in a no-decision for him. Calculating the pitching runs, we find that Johnson leads these four pitchers with a pitching runs total of 56.67. Jim Palmer's 1975 season netted 51.32 runs, followed by Bret Saberhagen's 1985 season (33.46 runs), and Bartolo Colon's 2005 season (only 17.57 runs). It is interesting to see that Palmer lost eleven games but still had an ERA of about two runs per game (his ten shutouts averaged out his losses).

Fielding Runs

Back to Earl Weaver's theorem for winning ballgames. After good pitching, a team should be able to execute the fundamentals of the game. Part of that involves defense. Weaver's Baltimore Orioles teams always had players winning Gold Glove Awards for being the best at their respective defensive positions. He and other managers would sacrifice a good bat for a good glove, especially for middle infielders. Consider second basemen Davey Johnson (3 Gold Gloves, .261 BA) and Bobby Grich (4 Gold Gloves, .266 BA), shortstop Mark Belanger (8 Gold Gloves, .228 BA), third baseman Brooks Robinson (a record 16 Gold Gloves, .267 BA), center fielder Paul Blair (8 Gold Gloves, .250 BA), and pitcher Jim Palmer (4 Gold Gloves). They all flashed their leather for the Orioles. Luis Aparicio won three of his eight Gold Gloves playing shortstop for the Orioles before Belanger came along. How does this defense transform into runs? Thorn and Palmer developed a defensive-runs formula, based on linear weights.

What if each Gold Glove Award recipient was replaced with an average fielder who was a better hitter? How many runs might not be saved? Is the fielding percentage of a player the best measure for defensive skills? The linear-weights fielding-runs formula for second basemen, shortstops and third basemen involves calculating a league average for each position, followed by a rating for the team in question at each position. The Pirates' Bill Mazeroski set the defensive runs record for infielders with 46.5 in 1963. The average position relative to the league, is given by

$$\text{Average position league} = \frac{0.20 \times [PO + (2 \times A) - E + DP] \text{league at position}}{PO \text{ league total} - K \text{ league total}}$$

where PO = putouts, A = assists, E = errors, DP = double plays, and K = strikeouts. Then the team rating is given by

$$\text{Team Runs per position} = 0.20 \times [PO + (2 \times A) - E + DP] \text{team at position} -$$
$$\text{Average position league} \times (\text{team PO} - \text{team K})$$

Notice that the coefficient for assists is two; assists are doubly weighted because more skill is required to get an assist than to record a putout. Individual players are evaluated by prorating the putouts. In 1971, Mark Belanger recorded 280 putouts in 149 games at shortstop for Baltimore. The Orioles as a team recorded 297 putouts at the shortstop position. Thus, Belanger would get credit for 280/297 = 94.3 percent of the putouts made at short. Using the formulas above, the Orioles shortstop rating in 1971 was 14.25 runs, so Belanger gets credit for 0.943 × 14.25 = 13.43 runs. This left Earl Weaver in a position to decide whether Mark Belanger's glove was worth more runs than his bat. (Coincidentally, the Blade batted .266 in 1971, 38 points higher than his career average.)

For catchers, Thorn and Palmer modified the defensive linear weights fielding runs by taking strikeouts away from the catchers' putouts. For first basemen, double plays and putouts were taken away, as they require much less fielding skill except in an occasional instance. This leaves only 0.20 × (2 A – E) in the formula's numerator. For outfielders, the formula for linear weights is 0.20 × (PO + 4 A – E + 2 DP). Thorn and Palmer conjectured that the "weighting for assists was boosted here because a good outfielder can prevent runs through the threat of assists that are never made; for outfielders, the assist is essentially an elective play." They counted the three outfielders on each team with the most putouts. The top putout player is designated the center fielder, and then the other two's totals are pooled. League averages from each group are obtained, and the center fielders are compared to the average for center fielders, whereas the left and right fielders are compared to averages for those positions. There might be a source of error in the calculations, as late-inning substitutes for outfielders make it difficult to count the exact number of innings a player plays. Finally, for defensive runs for pitchers, the innings are known and no problem arises. For pitchers, the outfielder's formula is modified to subtract individual pitcher strikeouts from the total number of potential outs (to help great strikeout pitchers like Nolan Ryan or Randy Johnson). Further, pitchers' chances are weighted less than infielders' assists, which might account for the difference between fly ball and ground ball pitchers.. Thus the formula for pitchers is 0.10 × (PO + 2 A – E + DP).

Armed with this strategy for defensive comparison, we can make an argument for who the greatest defensive catcher of all time might be. In any discussion on catching defense, Johnny Bench is a name that should be included. The fourteen-time National League All-Star won ten Gold Glove Awards as the backstop for the Cincinnati Reds. He established the standard by winning the award every year from 1968 through 1977. In addition, he won the Rookie of the Year Award in 1968 and two Most Valuable Player Awards. His Hall of Fame plaque begins, "Redefined standards by which catchers are measured." Bench's career fielding percentage as a catcher was

.990, which exceeds the league fielding percentage of .987 over the 17 seasons in which Bench played. Was he the best ever?

Since 1992, Ivan Rodriguez has been recognized as one of the best catchers in the major leagues. From 1992 through 2001, Rodriguez also won ten consecutive Gold Glove Awards, and he has won two more since then, in 2004 and 2006. His twelve awards are a record. He has been named to 13 All-Star squads, has won the American League Most Valuable Player Award (1999), and he sports a career fielding percentage of .991, compared to a league average of .991 over his 16 seasons.

Johnny Bench committed 97 errors in 1742 games as a catcher; through 2006, Ivan Rodriguez had committed 117 errors in 1934 games behind the plate. In his career, Bench had 9249 put-outs and 850 assists; through 16 seasons, Rodriguez had 11676 put-outs and 989 assists. Bench has a career range factor of 5.80 (compared to a league range factor of 5.59); Rodriguez has a career range factor of 6.55 (compared to a league range factor of 5.94). Can we compare them using Fielding Runs? Table 7.5 gives the defensive statistics in tabular form.

	G	PO	A	E	DP
Bench	1742	9249	850	97	127
Rodriguez	1934	11676	989	117	128

Table 7.5 Defensive statistics for Bench and Rodriguez

For catchers' fielding runs, Thorn and Palmer remove strikeouts from their put-outs. If they didn't, this statistic wouldn't make a whole lot of sense, as it would give credit to pitchers instead of catchers. Unfortunately, that requires that a game-by-game breakdown for each catcher-pitcher pair be conducted, to ensure that each catcher gets credit only for those strikeouts which he caught. That data is not readily available on the web. What to do? We offer a better statistic, "win shares," which will be reviewed in Inning 7.

As a wrap-up to this chapter, let's study the career of Jim Kaat. Jim Kitty Kaat was signed by the Washington Senators as an amateur free-agent pitcher in 1957. He debuted in the major leagues for the Senators on August 2, 1959. Over 25 seasons, Kaat pitched for six different big-league teams, finishing his career with a record of 283–237. At his retirement, those 283 victories placed Kaat twentieth on the all-time career victories list (he is now thirtieth). His 898 games played ranks nineteenth all-time among pitchers, and only Cy Young has more games played among pitchers who were primarily starters. Kaat averaged over 27 starts per season (over 25 years). Three times he topped the 20-win mark, three times he was voted to the American League All-Star team, and just once he received votes for the Cy Young Award (finishing 4th in voting in 1975). In addition to being a dependable pitcher, Kitty was an excellent fielder. He won sixteen Gold Glove Awards in consecutive years from 1962 through 1977 (that is second best all-time). Finally, he hit .185 in 1004 at-bats, with 16 home runs and 106 RBIs. Not bad for a pitcher.

Taking these statistics into account, let's determine the number of pitching runs and fielding runs that Kaat provided his teams. In the tables below we provide his pitching and fielding statistics.

W	L	G	GS	IP	H	R	ER	ERA	LgERA
283	237	898	625	4530.3	4620	2038	1738	3.45	3.69

Table 7.6 Jim Kaat's pitching statistics

G	PO	A	E	DP	Inn
898	262	744	56	65	4530

Table 7.7 Jim Kaat's fielding statistics

Using this information, we see that his pitching runs can be determined as

$$\text{Pitching Runs} = \frac{\text{Innings Pitched} \times (\text{League ERA} - \text{Pitcher's ERA})}{9}$$

$$= \frac{4530 \times (3.69 - 3.45)}{9}$$

$$= 120.81$$

So, over 25 seasons, Jim Kaat prevented 121 more runs than an average pitcher would have given the same number of IP. Although he had fifteen seasons with a winning percentage above .500, and he finished with a .544 winning percentage, he averaged about a half win per season which he contributed to his teams' successes.

Defensively, recall that as long as the number of innings are known, the linear-weights measure for fielding runs can be calculated with little difficulty.

Easy Tosses

1. The 1971 Baltimore Orioles had four starting pitchers who won at least 20 games that season. The statistics for Mike Cuellar, Pat Dobson, Jim Palmer, and Dave McNally are listed below. Calculate the pitching runs for

each hurler. Given their statistics below, who contributed the most pitching wins for the Orioles that year? The league earned run average was 3.36 runs.

	ERA	W	L	CG	SHO	IP	H	R	ER
Mike Cuellar	3.08	20	9	21	4	292.3	250	111	100
Pat Dobson	2.90	20	8	18	4	282.3	248	104	91
Jim Palmer	2.68	20	9	20	3	282.0	231	94	84
Dave McNally	2.89	21	5	11	1	224.3	188	75	72

2. Pete Alexander (1916), George Bradley (1876), Jack Coombs (1910), and Bob Gibson (1968) are the only pitchers in history with thirteen or more shutouts in a single season. Alexander also had twelve (1915) and nine twice (1913 and 1919). Calculate their pitching runs.

	ERA	W	L	CG	SHO	IP	H	R	ER	LgERA
Alexander	1.55	33	12	38	16	389.0	323	90	67	2.64
Bradley	1.23	45	19	63	16	573.0	470	229	78	2.15
Coombs	1.30	31	9	35	13	353.0	248	74	51	2.37
Gibson	1.12	22	9	28	13	304.7	198	49	38	2.90

Note: According to *Baseball-reference.com*, George Bradley gave up 229 runs in 1876, but only 78 were earned! That equates to almost 75 percent of his runs being unearned.

3. In 1999, Rafael Palmiero won his third Gold Glove Award as a first baseman. Interestingly, he only played 28 games at first base (he played 135 games as a designated hitter). Compare his fielding runs to five other American League first basemen from 1999.

4. We have seen that Jim Kaat was a great defensive pitcher, having won sixteen Gold Gloves in his career. From 1990 through 2006, Greg Maddux won the award for National League pitchers every year but once (2003, when his teammate Mike Hampton won the award), tying Kaat's total of 16. Bob Gibson won the coveted defensive award nine consecutive times (from 1965 through 1973). Who contributed a higher average of fielding runs per season, "Mad Dog" Maddux or "Gibby" Gibson?

Hard Sliders

1. Eddie Murray is the only first baseman to win multiple Gold Glove Awards in the American League and be elected into the Hall of Fame.

Compare the fielding runs of the players who have won seven or more Gold Glove Awards. Each is listed below with a season in which his fielding percentage was highest. Compare the fielding runs to each player's batting runs for the season.

	Year	Tm	G	PO	A	E	DP	FP	lgFP	RFg	lgRFg
Keith Hernandez	1985	NYM	157	1310	139	4	113	0.997	0.993	9.23	8.54
Don Mattingly	1993	NYY	130	1258	84	3	123	0.998	0.993	10.32	8.24
George Scott	1973	MIL	157	1388	118	9	144	0.994	0.992	9.59	8.27
Vic Power	1960	CLE	147	1177	145	5	145	0.996	0.991	8.99	8.04
Bill White	1964	STL	160	1513	101	6	125	0.996	0.990	10.09	8.83

2. Fernando Valenzuela won both the Rookie of the Year Award and Cy Young Award in 1981 (and he placed 5th in the Most Valuable Player voting). Baseball writers often discuss the sophomore jinx; i.e., after a great rookie season, a player has a sub-par second year. Using the *Linear Weights Pitching Runs*, compare the rookie and sophomore seasons for the following National League pitchers: Valenzuela (1981, 1982), Dwight Gooden (1984, 1985), Hideo Nomo (1995, 1996), and Dontrelle Willis (2003, 2004).

Inning 6:
The Runs-Created School

In Inning 4, we explored Pete Palmer's linear-weights system to analyze a player's offensive performance. The model is based on how many runs beyond average that a player produces. Thus, an average player scored zero, and below average players have negative linear weights.

In the 1970s, a night watchman at the Stokely Van Camp factory in Lawrence, Kansas, studied baseball box scores long into the night. His name was Bill James, and his self-published books filled with his findings and occasional iconoclastic rants won him a small but loyal following. His yearly books, entitled *The Baseball Abstract,* started being published for a mass audience in 1982.

He determined that the primary purpose of an offense is the creation of runs, and sought formulas that best described how many runs a particular player can be credited as having created.

In his 1985 *Baseball Abstract,* James set forth his offensive philosophy in axiomatic form:

- Axiom I: A ballplayer's purpose in playing baseball is to do those things which create wins for his team, while avoiding those things which create losses for his team.

- Axiom II: Wins result from runs scored. Losses result from runs allowed.

- First Corollary to Axiom II: An offensive player's job is to create runs for his team.

James quantified the relationship stated in Axiom 2 with the Pythagorean Record, a formula that predicts winning percentage based solely on runs scored by a team and runs allowed.

The Pythagorean Record is $\dfrac{(RS)^x}{(RS)^x + (RA)^x}$, where RS is the number of runs a team has scored and RA is the number that it has allowed. The exponent x is an as yet undetermined quantity. In the formula's earliest incarnation, James used $x = 2$ as the exponent, but other formulas exist that change the exponent in such a way to improve the accuracy of the projection. Some of these include $x = 1.81$, $x = 1.83$, or x to be determined by a formula that incorporates the team's runs scored and allowed.

The 1969 San Francisco Giants had a record of 92–70, a winning percentage of .556. They scored 713 runs while allowing 636. Using the Pythagorean Record with $x = 2$, i.e.,

$$\frac{(RS)^2}{(RS)^2 + (RA)^2} \text{, we have } \frac{(713)^2}{(713)^2 + (636)^2} = \frac{508369}{508369 + 404496} = 0.557.$$

The 1969 Houston Astros scored 8 more runs than they allowed during the season, 676 to 668, the smallest margin in the NL that year. For Houston, these totals predict a winning percentage of

$$\frac{(676)^2}{(676)^2 + (668)^2} = \frac{456976}{465976 + 446224} = 0.505,$$

which translated to 82 (actually, 81.9) wins in a 162 game season. The Astros in 1969 were 81–81.

Using this formula, it would be mathematically impossible for a team that scores more runs than it allows to have a winning percentage below .500, and a team that scores fewer runs than it allows to have a winning percentage above .500. Of course, this could happen in real life, and in fact, this formula can serve as a testament to (or an indictment of) the abilities of the team's manager to influence his team's record.

In 1969, only three teams outplayed their Pythagorean Records, and three others were less than one win below it. Two teams were more than 6 wins better, the eventual World Champion Mets, managed by Gil Hodges, and the expansion San Diego Padres, managed by Preston Gomez. The Dodgers, managed by Walter Alston, were the most wins (7) below the projection for the year.

Runs Created

In order to get a feel for how many runs a player can be credited with actually having produced, Bill James devised a model called runs created (RC). The most basic version of the runs created formula is

$$\frac{(H + BB) \times (TB)}{AB + BB}.$$

Beautiful in its simplicity, this formula can predict effectively the number of runs a league will score in a given season. This model usually predicts a run total within several percent of the actual total. In many of baseball's earliest seasons, the four quantities needed for this formula are the only ones available.

In 1986, the 12 teams in the National League scored a total of 8096 runs.

The four quantities in the RC formula were

AB	*H*	*BB*	*TB*
65730	16643	6560	24977

Table 8.1 The 1986 NL totals

Thus, we have $RC = \dfrac{(6560 + 16643) \times 24977}{65730 + 6560} = 8017$, which is within 1 percent of the actual run total.

Alternatively, this can be computed as OB × SLG × AB, or OB × TB. James stated the following as a "Known Principle of Sabermetrics":

• There are two essential elements to an offense: its ability to get on base, and its ability to advance runners.

In the RC, the first part of the numerator, the H + BB, is the "on base" portion of the formula, while the second part of the numerator, the TB, represents the "advancement" part. The denominator is roughly the number of opportunities.

Note that there are elements an offense not included in the RC formula. For that reason, we will refer to this version as basic runs created (BRC).

Two of the most glaring figures absent from the BRC formula are the stolen base and the caught stealing. There are other elements missing (HBP, for example) that will be considered in other versions of the formula. However, the formula will always take on the basic form of

$$\frac{A \times B}{C},$$

where A represents the on-base portion, B represents the advancement portion, and C represents opportunities.

Thus, to incorporate stolen bases, we first must consider the impact of a failed stolen base attempt, caught stealing (CS). It seems that CS statistics needs to be subtracted from the on-base portion, but added to the opportunity portion. Thus, A = H + BB − CS, while C = AB + BB + CS. Now, to consider the advancement value of a stolen base, James decided not to count a stolen base as being equal to a base gained via hitting. Instead, B = TB + (0.7 × SB). In his *1982 Baseball Abstract*, James gave two reasons for this adjustment:

1. A stolen base advances only one runner; each base hit advances the batter as a runner and anyone else who happens to be aboard.

2. If you used 1.0 at the value for each SB, the formula would no longer work; it would no longer predict actual run totals.

Let us apply this new version of the runs created formula, which we will call Stolen Base Runs Created (SBRC), where SBRC =

$$\frac{(H + BB - CS) \times (TB + (0.7 \times SB))}{AB + BB + CS},$$

to the National League in 1986. Table 8.2 shows the league numbers with the stolen base considerations.

AB	H	BB	SB	CS	TB
65730	16643	6560	1842	858	24977

Table 8.2 1986 NL totals, including stolen base considerations

$$\text{SBRC} = \frac{(6560 + 16643 - 858) \times (24977 + 0.07 \times (1842))}{65730 + 6560 + 858} = 8119.$$

This adjusted number, is only one quarter of one percent, or 23 runs, higher than the actual total runs scored that year incredibly close, given that there are only 6 elements to the formula.

It is easy to see that with some refinement the formula could be made even more precise; however, not every statistic is available for every season. Nonetheless, if one has access to GIDP, IBB (intentional walks), SH (sacrifice hits), SF (sacrifice flies), and HBP (hit by pitch), then these can be incorporated into $\frac{A \times B}{C}$ as follows:

• A = H + BB − CS + HBP − GIDP

• B = TB + [0.26 (TBB − IBB + HBP)] + [0.52 (SH + SF + SB)]

• C = AB + BB + HBP + SH + SF

James referred to this formula as the technical version of runs created, which we will call RCTECH. The added statistics for the 1986 NL were obtained from the *Stats Inc. Handbook*:

HBP	SH	SF	IBB	GIDP
312	869	519	803	1360

Table 8.3 Additional factors for the NL 1986

So, for RCTECH,

A = 16643 + 6560 − 858 + 312 − 1360 = 21297
B = 24997 + [0.26(24977 − 803 + 312)] + [0.52(869 + 519 + 1842)] = 33043
C = 65730 + 6560 + 312 + 869 + 519 = 73990
and

$$\frac{A \times B}{C} = \frac{21297 \times 33043}{73990} = 8127,$$

which is within four tenths of one percent of the actual run total. It is unusual that the formula that uses less data turns out to be more accurate than the more involved model.

There are now twenty-four versions of the runs-created formula based largely on the statistics available for a particular season. They are all listed in the *Stats Inc. Handbook.*

For the American League's 1923 season, the H, BB, AB and TB stats are all available:

AB	H	BB	SB	CS	TB
42068	11876	4092	741	607	16318

Table 8.4 1923 AL totals

so BRC = $\dfrac{(11876 + 4092) \times (16318)}{(42068 + 4092)}$ = 5645, within 5 percent of the actual runs total, 5887.

In addition, HBP, K, SB and CS are available, and players were then credited with a sacrifice hit any time a fly out advanced a runner, not just those on third, so that will affect some of the factors. The same data was available for the NL that year, and this formula, HDG12, is used for both leagues in 1915 as well as 1920–1925. HDG12 has the following formula:

A = H + BB + HBP − CS
B = 0.98(TB) + [0.25(BB + HBP)] + [0.46(SB + SH)]
C = AB + BB + HBP + SH

The raw data for the AL in 1923 is presented here:

2B	3B	HR	AB	H	BB	SB	CS	TB	HBP	SH
2010	553	442	42068	11876	4092	741	607	16318	341	1617

Table 8.5 Additional 1923 AL totals

The HBP and SH data come from the *Stats Inc. Handbook.*

Using the basic runs created formula, the runs-created estimate is within 5 percent of the actual runs total. It can easily be verified that the HDG12 runs created estimate is 5934, so we are now within 1 percent of the total.

The formula used for the 1986 NL is HDG23. Included are sacrifice flies and grounded into double plays. Strikeouts are also incorporated; that year saw NLers establish a new record for number of strikeouts, striking out almost 1000 times more than the previous season.

The runs-created formulas, with some modifications and specifications, can be applied to individual players. In 1986, Mike Schmidt was the Most Valuable Player in the National League, scoring 97 runs and driving in 119. How does that translate into real run production for Philadelphia that season?

Continuing the axiomatic thread of James' presentation, he states that "the objective of a player is to produce runs," and "actual runs and RBI are too dependent on external factors." Thus, runs created, in attempting to determine the number of runs for which a particular player can be credited, attempts to do so in a situation-neutral context.

Here are Schmidt's 1986 MVP numbers:

2B	3B	HR	AB	H	BB	SB	CS	TB	HBP	SH	SF	IBB	GIDP	SO
29	1	37	552	160	89	1	2	302	7	0	9	25	8	84

Table 8.6 Mike Schmidt's 1986 statistics

$A = H + BB + HBP - CS - GIDP = 160 + 89 + 7 - 2 - 8 = 246$

$B = TB + [0.26 (TBB - IBB + HBP)] + [0.52 (SH + SF + SB)]$
$\quad = 302 + [0.26 (89 - 25 + 7)] + [0.52 (0 + 9 + 84)] = 368.82$

$C = AB + BB + HBP + SH + SF = 552 + 89 + 7 + 0 + 9 = 657$

which works out to a BRC of 117.3 and a TECHRC of 121.94.

James' Third Axiom of Sabermetrics reads: "All offense and defense occurs within a context of outs." To provide this context, James developed the concept of Offensive Winning Percentage (OWP), in which outs are a kind of "currency" paid to produce runs. A more efficient player, therefore, will produce runs using fewer outs, and theoretically, if two players create the same number of runs, the tie can be broken by compared by how few outs they spend. In a 162-game season, at 27 outs per game, a team will have a basis of 4374 outs. Extra innings, rain-shortened, and unplayed games might change that total, but this is the starting point.

Continuing the analysis of Mike Schmidt, we see that he contributed 409 outs, a figure determined by taking AB – H, and adding SH and SF, outs not counted in the original total. We also add his 8 GIDP, as these are additional outs he caused. These 409 outs translates to 409 / 27 or 15 games (actually, 15.1). The National League in 1986 averaged 4.18 runs per team per game, slightly lower than the usual historical figure of 4.5. On the other hand, at 15.1 games, Schmidt produced 117.3 / 15.1 = 7.74 runs per game using BRC, and 121.94 / 15.1 = 8.05 runs per game using TECHRC. If we put these figures into the Pythagorean Record, we obtain

$$\frac{(7.74)^2}{(7.74)^2 + (4.18)^2} = 0.774$$

for the basic version, and

$$\frac{(8.05)^2}{(8.05)^2 + (4.18)^2} = 0.788$$

for the technical version.

What this means is that a team of nine Mike Schmidts at the plate, given average pitching and defensive support for the year 1986, would have produced a winning percentage of .774 (or 125 wins) or .788 (128 wins) over the course of the 162-game season. For his 15-game "season," Schmidt's offensive win-loss record would round to 12–3 using either winning percentage.

Many fans of the New York Mets would dispute the MVP selection of Schmidt in 1986. However, the player on the Mets with the highest runs created numbers was Keith Hernandez. His 1986 statistics are listed here:

2B	3B	HR	AB	H	BB	SB	CS	TB	HBP	SH	SF	IBB	GIDP	SO
34	1	13	551	160	94	2	1	75	4	0	15	9	21	63

Table 8.7 Keith Hernandez's 1986 statistics

which yield BRC = 101.07 and TECHRC = 103.41 (you can verify these numbers).

Hernandez used 427 outs, or 16 (15.8) games. You can verify that for the same season, given average pitching and defensive support, a team of nine Keith Hernandezes at bat would have a winning percentage of .700 (BRC) or .710 (TECHRC), 113 or 115 wins in a 162 game season, or a 11–5 record for his 16 games. Thus, those Mets fans who would make Hernandez's MVP case might be on the wrong track.

HDG23, used for both AL and NL data between from 1955 to 1988, has the following formula:

A = H + BB + HBP – CS – GIDP
B = TB + [0.29 (BB + HBP – IBB)] + [0.53 (SF + SH)] + [0.64 (SB)] – 0.03 (K)
C = AB + BB + HBP + SH + SF

Note how it differs slightly from HDG22, which is used only for the major leagues in 1954:

A = H + BB+ HBP – CS – GIDP
B = 0.98 (TB) + [0.24 (BB + HBP)] + [0.5 (SF + SH)] + [0.62 (SB)] –
    0.03 (K)
C = AB + BB + HBP + SH + SF

The main difference in the two years is the recording of intentional walks after 1954.

So, for 1986, factoring in the 11648 strikeouts that year, the totals for HDG23 are: A 21297, B 28302, C 73990 or (21297 × 28302) / 73990 = 8146, within ⅔ of a percentage point of the actual run total.

Since the publication of the 24 HDG runs-created formulas, James has introduced some nuances that bring more situational numbers into the formula, including home runs with the bases empty. However, as always, any element is included because it makes the league estimate more accurate. In one adjustment to the RC formulas, James suggests introducing some coefficients to the A, B and C quantities. Thus, a more accurate runs-created formula, putting the individual player's numbers into the context of a team, would be

$$\frac{(A+2.4)\times(B+3C)}{9C}-0.9C.$$

Expanded out, and factoring out the 9, yields

$$\frac{1}{9}\left[\frac{A\times B}{C}+(2.4)B+(3)A-(0.9)C\right],$$

which seems to weight the individual's numbers as one-ninth of a team's offense. The other coefficients are unexplained, except that possibly they were arrived at via trial and error using norms throughout baseball history.

In any case, Schmidt's numbers for HDG23 were A = 246, B = 325.48, and C = 657, so

$$\frac{1}{9}\left[\frac{A\times B}{C}+(2.4)B+(3)A-(0.9)C\right]=$$

$$\frac{1}{9}\left[\frac{246\times325.48}{657}+(2.4)(325.48)+(3)(246)-(0.9)(657)\right]=$$

$$\frac{1}{9}\left[121.87+781.15+738-591.3\right]=$$

$$\frac{1}{9}\left[1049.7\right]=116.64,$$

a value that is about 1 run lower than his BRC estimate. Using these coefficients, Keith Hernandez's runs estimate drops to 97.7.

The formula used for both leagues since 1988 is HDG24. It is slightly different from HDG23, and includes adjustments for home runs with men on base and for hitting with men in scoring position.

Easy Tosses

1. Here are some numbers for the American League in 1998:

	Games	*Runs*	*Opp Runs*	*W*	*L*
NYY	162	965	656	114	48
TEX	162	940	871	88	74
BOS	162	876	729	92	70
SEA	161	859	855	76	85
CHW	163	861	931	80	82
CLE	162	850	779	89	73
BAL	162	817	785	79	83
TOR	163	816	768	88	74
OAK	162	804	866	74	88
ANA	162	787	783	85	77
MIN	162	734	818	70	92
DET	162	722	863	65	97
KC	161	714	899	72	89
TB	162	620	751	63	99

(a) Determine the Pythagorean Records for the Texas Rangers (TEX) and the Toronto Blue Jays (TOR). Each team won 88 games that year.

(b) Compute the Pythagorean Record for the remaining teams in the American League for 1998. Note that the number of runs and wins do not balance out, as there was interleague play. The AL scored 11 more runs than it allowed in 1998. Which team played the farthest above its projection, and which played the farthest below?

2. If you were told that the American League in 1998 had 78,416 at-bats, 21,276 hits, 4248 doubles, 408 triples, 2499 home runs and 7737 bases on balls, how many runs would such a league be expected to score? How does this compare with the league's actual runs total (see question 1)?

3. Bobby Murcer in 1971 had the following statistics:

AB	*R*	*H*	*2B*	*3B*	*HR*	*RBI*	*SB*	*CS*	*BB*	*SO*	*SH*	*SF*	*IBB*	*HBP*	*GDP*
529	94	175	25	6	25	94	14	8	91	60	1	3	13	0	9

Calculate his BRC, SBRC, and TECHRC.

4. In the questions following chapter 4, you were asked to compare the contenders for the 1983 AL MVP award, Orioles teammates Cal Ripken Jr. and Eddie Murray, by their Linear Weights scores. Using HDG23, and the correction,

$$\frac{\left(A+(2.4\times C)\right)\times\left(B+(3\times C)\right)}{9\times C}-0.9C$$

determine who had the better offensive season.

Player	AB	H	2B	3B	HR	BB	HBP	SB	CS	HBP	SH	SF	IBB	GDP	K
Cal Ripken	663	211	47	2	27	58	0	0	4	0	0	5	0	24	97
Eddie Murray	582	178	30	3	33	86	3	5	1	3	0	9	13	13	90

5. The Seattle Mariners won an amazing 116 regular season games in 2001. Calculate the expected number of wins based on the Pythagorean Record (with $x = 1.82$), using their RA and RS at the end of each month of the season. The data is listed below:

Month	W	L	RS	RA
April	20	5	138	89
May	20	7	172	126
June	18	9	170	131
July	18	9	135	87
August	20	9	153	103
September	15	6	115	76
October	5	1	44	15

What happens when you change the value of the exponent (x) to be exactly 2?

Hard Sliders

1. As in chapter 4, the table below lists the statistics for the top five home run hitters of all time, for the season in which each won his first Most Valuable Player Award: Hank Aaron in 1957, Barry Bonds in 1991, Babe Ruth in 1923, Willie Mays in 1954, and Sammy Sosa in 1998.

a. Calculate runs created using the appropriate formula. For Aaron, Bonds and Sosa, use HDG23, for Mays, use HDG22, and for Ruth, use HDG12.

b. Calculate the number of outs for which each player was responsible, and then calculate the number of "games" for each. In the case of Bonds, Sosa,

Ruth and Aaron, use a divisor of 27 for games. For Ruth, use 25.5, as all outs are not accounted for in the available statistics.

c. Divide the runs-created total in a. by the games total in b. to obtain RC/27outs figure. How do the players rank?

Player	Year	AB	H	2B	3B	HR	BB	HBP	SB	CS	HBP	SH	SF	IBB	GDP	K
Aaron	1957	615	198	27	6	44	57	0	1	1	0	0	3	15	13	58
Bonds	1990	519	156	32	3	33	93	3	52	13	3	0	6	15	8	83
Ruth	1923	522	205	45	13	41	170	4	17	21	4	3	n/a	n/a	n/a	93
Mays	1954	565	195	33	13	41	66	12	8	5	2	0	7	n/a	12	57
Sosa	1998	643	198	20	0	66	73	1	18	9	1	0	5	14	20	171

2. In question (2) above, you were asked to calculate Bobby Murcer's runs-created totals. Calculate his RC again, this time using HDG23 and the correction

$$\frac{\left(A+(2.4\times C)\right)\times\left(B+(3\times C)\right)}{9\times C} - 0.9C.$$

Given that the AL in 1971 averaged 3.87 runs per game, calculate Bobby Murcer's offensive winning percentage.

3. Mark McGwire was voted the American league's Rookie of the Year in 1987 when he hit a rookie record 49 home runs, drove in 118 runs and slugged .618 Compare Big Mac's runs created using both the BRC, the RCTECH, and the HDG23.

Inning 7: Win Shares

Shortcomings in Runs Created

Honest to a fault, Bill James recognized some flaws in his runs-created system and he expounded on them in *The New Bill James Historical Baseball Abstract*. Among the most egregious, in his opinion, was the need for the number to be placed into a team context. Recall that the BRC formula

$$\text{BRC} = \frac{(H + BB) \times (TB)}{AB + BB},$$

accurately predicts a team's runs to within 5 percent, and the adjustments for statistics available in a given season usually moves the estimate to well within 1 percent.

James used the following examples to illustrate what he asserts was one of the shortcomings: Player A and B play on Team 1. Each has 400 AB + BB, 150 TB, and 150 H + BB, for BRC = (150)(150) / 400 = 56.25, or a total for the two of them of 112.25, which matches the sum of their accomplishments 800|300|300 for BRC = (300)(300) / 800 = 112.5.

However, consider Player C and Player D on Team 2. Player C has 400 AB + BB, 100 TB, and 100 H + BB, or BRC = (100)(100) / 400 = 25. Player D has 400 AB + BB, 200 TB, and 200 H + BB, with BRC = (200)(200) / 400 = 100. Their total BRC as a sum of the individuals is 125, but their aggregate totals match the players from Team 1, 800|300|300 and BRC = 112.5. If at all possible, the whole should equal the sum of its parts.

Another observation from James is that, if two players each steal 10 bases, but one is a better hitter than the other, the runs-created formula will compute that the stolen bases created more runs for the better hitter, simply because the multiplier is larger.

To correct these "problems," the adjustments for the runs-created formula essentially creates a typical team, figures out how many runs the team would create with the player, how many runs the team would create without the player, and subtracts one from the other.

Recall that the correction is: $\dfrac{1}{9}\left[\dfrac{A \times B}{C} + (2.4)B + (3)A - (0.9)C\right]$

The numbers for Players A and B remain unchanged by this correction, but the numbers for the Team 2 players are given in Table 9.1.

	C	A	B	BRC	ADJ
Player C	400	100	100	25	22.78
Player D	400	200	200	100	91.11

Table 9.1 Runs created with adjustment

Thus, the Team 2 players' individual total adds up roughly to 114, and James contends that the adjustment eliminates the problem of interaction between the run elements.

Other adjustments in the runs-created formula deal with situational statistics. In James' opinion, the two that have the greatest impact on runs scored are batting average with runners in scoring position and home runs with men on base (as opposed to bases-empty HR). Thus, these are brought into the RC formula.

The final adjustment comes when the sum of the individual RC is significantly greater (or less) than the team's runs scored. For example, a 5 percent discrepancy in either direction will bring a commensurate 5 percent raising (or lowering) of each individual's RC.

From this context, James then developed his new rating system, Win Shares.

Win Shares: An Overview

The "win shares" concept is the latest in James' quest for the perfect evaluation system. Essentially, a team's wins are multiplied by three, and then the individual players are assigned a portion of that total based on hitting/base running, fielding, and pitching contributions. Roughly 48 percent of the available win shares are assigned to the first category, 17 percent to the second, and 35 percent to the third.

For individuals, a 30 win share season is of MVP-caliber, and a season over 40 is historic. The pitchers pre–1893, many of whom pitched 400–500 innings per season, scored off the win-shares chart. James adjusted this by dividing these pitchers' totals by two, or else all of the top seasons in baseball history would have been concentrated in those players, a seemingly unlikely occurrence.

Selecting a random team from baseball history, the 1901 Philadelphia Phillies, second place finishers in the NL, went 83–57. Thus, 249 win-shares are available to be claimed. According to the 2002 book *Win Shares* by Bill James and Jim Henzler, 107.1 (43 percent) of the win shares were assigned for offense, 45.3 (18 percent) were assigned for fielding, and 96.6 (39 percent) were assigned for pitching.

The Phils were led by Hall of Fame outfielder Ed Delahanty's 33 win shares. This total tied him (along with Boston hurler Vic Willis and Brooklyn outfielder Jimmy Sheckard) for third in the NL. Jess Burkett at 38 and Honus Wagner at 37 paced the NL. The Philadelphia Athletics' Nap Lajoie (42) led the majors, and Baltimore's Cy Young was second in the AL with 41.

In Inning 6, we presented the Pythagorean formula, a way of predicting a team's record based on runs scored and allowed. In conjunction with win shares, James developed a concept known as marginal runs, another way to predict a team's record, based on the number of runs allowed less than the average and the number of runs scored greater than the league average. Thus, marginal runs are divided into two categories, offensive and defensive. On the offensive side, he defines a marginal run as any run scored by a team in excess of one-half the league average, i.e., team runs minus one-half the league average, or $R_{TEAM} - (0.5 \times R_{LGAVG}) = MR$. For defense, marginal runs are defined as each run allowed below 1.5 times the league average, or $(1.5 \times R_{LGAVG}) - RA_{TEAM}$.

In the National League in 1901, there were 5194 runs scored, and eight teams, which translates to an average of 649.25 runs per team. Thus, for the NL in 1901, we provide the marginal-runs calculations and totals in Table 9.2.

NL 1901	MR–O	MR–D	TOT
STL	467.5	284.5	752
PIT	451.5	439.5	891
BRO	419.5	373.5	793
PHI	343.5	430.5	774
CHC	253.5	274.5	528
CIN	236.5	155.5	392
NYG	219.5	218.5	438
BOS	206.5	417.5	624

Table 9.2 Marginal runs calculations for the NL, 1901

Marginal runs produce a prediction for winning percentage that is virtually identical to the Pythagorean Number. It allows for the marginal-runs concept to be the foundation for the win-shares method.

For the 1901 NL, the marginal-runs total is divided by twice the league average in runs scored. In 1901, the teams of the NL scored 5194 runs, which translates to an average of 649.25 for each team.

Dividing each team's marginal-runs total by 1298.5 gives a projected winning percentage, which, as in the Pythagorean Number, can be multiplied by the number of games played to arrive at a projected number of wins. Table 9.3 shows the projected wins for each team using each method.

NL 01	G	Wins	Pyth#	PythW	MR	MR %	MR W	diff Pytha	diff Marg
STL	142	76	0.569	81	752	0.579	82	5	6
PIT	140	90	0.679	95	891	0.686	96	5	6
BRO	137	79	0.606	83	793	0.611	84	4	5
PHI	140	83	0.602	84	774	0.596	83	1	0
CHC	140	53	0.406	57	528	0.407	57	4	4
CIN	142	52	0.320	45	392	0.302	43	7	9
NYG	141	52	0.342	48	438	0.337	48	4	4
BOS	140	69	0.477	67	624	0.481	67	2	2

Table 9.3 Comparison of actual wins, Pythagorean projection wins, and marginal-runs projection wins for NL, 1901

Even though the marginal-runs projected number of wins is no better than that of the Pythagorean projection (and, in some cases, significantly worse), there is a trade-off: marginal runs can be computed for each player using the ratio of marginal runs to wins. The normal ratio is approximately 9 to 1, regardless if the team is a good one or a bad one, although that number can vary. In 1901, for example, Cincinnati had 52 wins and 392 marginal runs (7.5:1), but the Reds outplayed their Pythagorean projection by 7 wins and their marginal-runs win projection by 9. Obviously, something was going on there. All the other teams were roughly within one of 9 (farthest away: Brooklyn 793 / 79 = 10.03).

Thus, using runs created, we can determine how many runs a player creates, separate out the marginal runs, and then, knowing the ratio of runs to wins, calculate the wins for each player. For pitchers, runs saved by an individual can be computed and then again, transformed into wins.

Win-Shares Calculation

In order to calculate win shares for a team, we will use the so-called "short form method" that James introduced in the *Win Shares* book. The long-form method is much more complicated, involving many more calculations and data, some of which is not readily available. We can compare the numbers we compute for the 1901 Phillies with the numbers James published in his book, which were obtained using the long-form method.

According to James, the short-form method seems to yield a value very close to that of the long form for years after 1920, and is fairly close to the long form for years prior to 1920.

Here is how to compute offensive win shares using the short form:
• Compute the outs made by each hitter
• Divide the outs by 12
• Subtract from the RC
• Divide by 3. If non-negative, then this is each hitter's batting WS
• If pitchers bat, repeat the process but don't subtract the outs

Thus, for the 1901 Phillies, we first compute the players' runs created, using the appropriate formula (for 1901, it is HDG-9).

	AB	R	H	2B	3B	HR	RBI	BB	HBP	SH	SB	RC HDG9
McFarland	295	33	84	14	2	1	32	18	0	3	11	40.3
Jennings	302	38	79	21	2	1	39	25	12	8	13	44.7
Hallman	445	46	82	13	5	0	38	26	4	29	13	29
Wolverton	379	42	117	15	4	0	43	22	6	6	13	57
Cross	483	49	95	14	1	1	44	52	5	7	24	43.8
Flick	540	112	180	32	17	8	88	52	7	13	30	132
Thomas	479	102	148	5	2	1	28	100	9	15	27	93.5
Delahanty	542	106	192	38	16	8	108	65	4	10	29	151
Barry	252	35	62	10	0	1	22	15	2	12	13	26.5
Slagle	183	20	37	6	2	1	20	16	3	7	5	16.9
Douglass	173	14	56	6	1	0	23	11	2	3	10	28.3
Jacklitsch	120	14	30	4	3	0	24	12	2	0	2	15.8
Dolan	37	0	3	0	0	0	2	2	0	0	0	0.46
Browne	26	2	5	1	0	0	4	1	1	0	2	2.09
Conn	18	2	4	1	0	0	0	0	1	0	0	1.35
Orth	128	14	36	6	0	1	15	3	1	0	3	15.2
Duggleby	115	10	19	2	1	0	5	3	1	3	2	4.97
Donahue	113	11	11	2	0	0	2	4	0	3	0	1.82
White	98	15	27	3	1	1	10	2	1	7	1	10.5
Townshend	64	2	7	1	1	0	5	0	1	0	1	1.43
Dunn	1	1	1	0	0	0	0	1	0	0	0	1.32

Table 9.4 Runs-created calculations for all batters
(including pitchers), 1901 Phillies

Then, for each non-pitcher, we calculate the number of outs made as a hitter. That would be, for the data available for NL 1901, AB − H + SH. This total is then divided by 12 and subtracted from the player's runs created total.

	McFarland	Jennings	Hallman	Wolverton	Cross	Flick	Thomas
Outs	265	272	428	343	441	441	392
RC-o/12	18.20	22.05	-6.69	28.38	7.03	95.21	60.79

	Delahanty	Barry	Slagle	Douglass	Jacklitsch	Dolan	Browne
Outs	446	229	170	162	106	37	24
RC-o/12	113.5	7.37	2.73	14.78	6.96	-2.62	0.09

	Conn	Orth	Duggleby	Donahue	White	Townshend	Dunn
Outs	16	114	108	105	90	62	0
RC-o/12	0.02	15.19	4.97	1.82	10.54	1.43	1.32

Table 9.5 Outs and runs created minus outs divided by 12 for non-pitchers, 1901 Phillies

Note that if a player's total is negative, he is assigned a value of zero for the next calculation. Also, there is no subtraction of "outs/12" for the pitchers as hitters (in the table, from Orth and down).

Finally, this total is divided by 3 to determine batting win shares. The results are here:

	McFarland	Jennings	Hallman	Wolverton	Cross	Flick	Thomas
BWS	6.07	7.35	0	9.46	2.34	31.74	20.26

	Delahanty	Barry	Jacklitsch	Dolan	Browne	Conn	Orth
BWS	37.83	2.46	2.32	0	0.03	0.01	5.06

	Duggleby	Donahue	White	Townshend	Dunn
BWS	1.66	0.61	3.52	0.48	0.44

Table 9.6 Batting win shares for the 1901 Phillies

This totals about 137 batting win shares for the 1901 Phillies. Note that a negative batting-win-shares total is entered as zero.

Using James' guideline of 48 percent of available wins shares for batters, we would need to assign 0.48 × 249, or approximately 119, of the win shares for offense. Our win-shares total of 137 is approximately 15 percent too high. However, an across-the-board 15 percent decrease per person would, with rounding-off, make the team's total too low.

In his calculation, using the long form, James assigned a total of 107 of the 1901 Phillies' win shares for batting. This is roughly 43 percent, not 48 percent. One reason is that the Phillies played in a hitters' park in 1901, inflating offensive statistics by 2 percent. The justification for a 5 percent reduction is not stated or clear.

We chose a reduction of 12.5 percent per player, and after rounding off, Table 9.7 shows how it reads:

	McFarland	Jennings	Hallman	Wolverton	Cross	Flick	Thomas
BWSrd	5	6	0	8	2	28	18

	Delahanty	Barry	Jacklitsch	Dolan	Browne	Conn	Orth
BWSrd	33	2	2	0	0	0	4

	Duggleby	Donahue	White	Townshend	Dunn
BWSrd	1	1	3	0	0

Table 9.7 Batting win shares, 1901 Phillies, reduced by 12.5 percent

For pitching win shares, the marginal-runs concept once again comes into play. In 1901, six men threw pitches for the Phillies, and their numbers are in Table 9.8.

	IP	R	ER	ERA
Orth	281.7	101	71	2.269
Duggleby	284.3	120	91	2.88
Donahue	295.3	111	85	2.59
White	236.7	122	84	3.194
Townshend	143.7	73	55	3.445
Dunn	4.7	16	11	21.21

Table 9.8 Pitching data for the 1901 Phillies

They let up a total of 543 runs, 397 of them earned, or 146 unearned runs. Thus, while the 1901 Phillies pitched to a 2.87 ERA, they gave up a total of 3.88 runs per game. In fact, this provides evidence that the Phillies were an above-average defensive team; the National league in 1901 scored 5194 runs, 3678 earned, for an average of 189.5 unearned runs per team, or more than fifty more unearned runs than the Phillies allowed.

By comparison, the 2001 edition of the Phillies had 22 men pitch, giving up 667 earned runs. The game certainly changed over the course of the century.

To calculate a team's pitching win shares, the league ERA is multiplied by 1.50, and then 1 is subtracted from this result. Then the number of earned runs the pitcher would have allowed had this been his ERA is computed.

For example, Al Orth had an ERA of 2.27, computed by multiplying earned runs (71) by 9 and dividing by the number of innings pitched (281⅔). The league ERA was 3.32; 1.5 × 3.32 – 1 = 3.98. To compute the number of earned runs Orth would have surrendered with this ERA, we take the standard ERA formula and solved for Earned Runs, i.e., ER = IP × ERA / 9. Thus, he would have given up (281⅔) × 3.98 / 9 = 124.6 projected ER. This total is then decreased by the actual number of earned runs allowed, so 124.6 – 71 = 53.6. Then his number of saves is added to this quantity, and then the total is divided by three. He had one save, so we have 54.6 / 3 = 18.2, or 18.2 win shares for Al Orth.

We note that Orth started 33 games in 1901, completed 30 of them, and had 20 wins, with an ERA more than a point below the league average. Roughly 18 win shares seems low for him; we will need to rectify this. But first, Table 9.9 gives the pitching win shares totals for the 1901 Phillies.

	IP	R	ER	ERA	LERA	*	SV	W	L	projER	projER – ER	PWS
Orth	281.7	101	71	2.27	3.32	3.98	1	20	12	124.6	53.6	18.2
Duggleby	284.3	120	91	2.88	3.32	3.98	0	20	12	125.7	34.7	11.6
Donahue	295.3	111	85	2.59	3.32	3.98	1	20	13	130.6	45.6	15.5
White	236.7	122	84	3.19	3.32	3.98	0	14	13	104.7	20.7	6.9
Townshend	143.7	73	55	3.45	3.32	3.98	0	9	6	63.53	8.5	2.8
Dunn	4.667	16	11	21.21	3.32	3.98	0	0	1	2.064	-8.9	0.0

Table 9.9 Data for calculating pitching win shares, 1901 Phillies
(*league ERA × 1.5 – 1)

Note that Jack Dunn's pitching win-shares total is actually –3; James treats any negative win shares as zero, although the folks at *Hardballtimes.com* allow for negative win shares.

Now, by James' formulation, pitching win shares should be 35 percent of the team's total, and 35 percent of 249 is about 87. The total pitching win shares is 55; this is about 63 percent of what the total should be. We adjust each pitcher's total upward by 37 percent. This adjustment still leaves the pitching win shares about 11 too low. So, recalling that the park factor favors hitters by 2 percent, we added 2 points to the total of each of the top five pitchers, after rounding off. This means that 85 of the 1901 Phillies win shares are assigned to pitching. James himself assigned 96, or approximately 38.5 percent.

	PWS - 137%	*PWS rounded & adjusted*
Orth	24.92	27
Duggleby	15.86	18
Donahue	21.28	23
White	9.43	11
Townshend	3.90	6
Dunn	0	0

Table 9.10 Pitching win shares, 1901 Phillies, adjusted and rounded

In the short-form method, calculating fielding win shares disregards defense by pitchers. Thus, we have win-shares totals for all the pitchers on the 1901 Phillies:

	WS-short	WS-long
Orth	32	29
Duggleby	20	22
Donahue	25	24
White	15	16
Townshend	7	8
Dunn	0	0

Table 9.11 Comparison of long- and short-form pitching win shares, 1901 Phillies

Note that the short form and long form totals are very similar.

James feels that his win-shares computation marks a breakthrough in valuation of players' defensive statistics. Among the factors and considerations that go into this analysis are the following:

1. Strikeouts are removed from catchers' fielding percentages;
2. First basemens' throwing arms can be evaluating by estimating the number of assists that are not simply 3–1 flips to the pitcher covering;
3. Ground balls by a team can be estimated;
4. Team double plays need to be adjusted for ground ball tendency and opponents' runners on base;
5. Putouts by third basemen do not indicate a particular skill level;
6. A bad team will have more outfielder and catcher assists than a good team.

Unfortunately, the short-form method takes none of these into account. Here is how to determine fielding win shares for position players:

• Catchers get 1 WS for every 24 G
• 1Bmen get 1 WS for every 76 G

- 2Bmen get 1 WS for every 28 G
- 3Bmen get 1 WS for every 38 G
- SS get 1 WS for every 25 G
- OFers get 1 WS for every 48 G

Here is the calculation for the 1901 Phillies:

	C	1B	2B	3B	SS	OF	FWS
McFarland	74						3
Jennings		80	1		1		1
Hallman			90	33			4
Wolverton				93			2
Cross					139		6
Flick						138	3
Thomas						129	3
Delahanty		58				84	3
Barry			35	16	1	13	1
Slagle						48	1
Douglass	41	6				2	2
Jacklitsch	30			1			1
Dolan			10				0
Browne						8	0
Conn			5				0
Orth						4	0
Duggleby							0
Donahue							0
White						1	0
Townshend						1	0
Dunn							0

Table 9.12 Fielding win shares, 1901 Phillies

Each total is rounded off. This totals 30 fielding win shares for the entire team; using James' guideline of 17 percent for fielding means that roughly 42 win shares (17 percent of 249) need to be assigned for fielding contributions. The total of 30 means that we are about 71 percent of where we need the figures to be; if we increase each total by 29 percent, and round off, we will have assigned about 39 Fielding Win Shares. If we assign each of the 5 pitchers who pitched a significant amount of time one fielding win share each for defensive contributions, after rounding-off we will have assigned 44 fielding win shares. James himself assigned 45 win shares for fielding. Our total is in shown here:

	McFarland	Jennings	Hallman	Wolverton	Cross	Flick
FWS rounded & adjusted	4	1	5	3	8	4

	Thomas	Delahanty	Barry	Dolan	Browne	Conn
FWS rounded & adjusted	4	4	1	0	0	0

	Orth	Duggleby	Donahue	White	Townshend	Dunn
FWS rounded & adjusted	1	1	1	1	1	0

Table 9.13 Fielding win shares, 1901 Phillies, rounded and adjusted

An individual player's win-shares total is computed by adding his pitching, batting and fielding win shares. This yields the entries here:

	McFarland	Jennings	Hallman	Wolverton	Cross	Flick	Thomas
WS	9	7	5	11	10	32	22

	Delahanty	Barry	Slagle	Douglass	Jacklitsch	Dolan	Browne
WS	37	3	2	7	3	0	0

	Conn	Orth	Duggleby	Donahue	White	Townshend	Dunn
WS	0	32	20	25	15	7	0

Table 9.14 Win-shares totals, 1901 Phillies

This totals 247, which is 2 short of 249. Looking at the un-rounded totals, it seems that Hughie Jennings and Shad Barry may have each deserved an extra win share, so they are awarded them. The last row of Table 9.15 shows the totals James obtained using the long-form method (the actual amount).

	McFarland	Jennings	Hallman	Wolverton	Cross	Flick	Thomas
WS	9	7	5	11	10	32	22
Final WS	9	8	5	11	10	32	22
Long Form	10	8	5	15	7	30	24

	Delahanty	Barry	Slagle	Douglass	Jacklitsch	Dolan	Browne
WS	37	3	2	7	3	0	0
Final WS	37	4	2	7	3	0	0
Long Form	33	4	3	7	4	0	0

	Conn	Orth	Duggleby	Donahue	White	Townshend	Dunn
WS	0	32	20	25	15	7	0
Final WS	0	32	20	25	15	7	0
Long Form	0	29	22	24	16	8	0

Table 9.15 Win shares, 1901 Phillies, with adjustment
for Jennings and Barry

Easy Tosses

1. Here are some numbers for the American League in 1998:

	Games	*Runs*	*Opp. Runs*	*W*	*L*
NYY	162	965	656	114	48
TEX	162	940	871	88	74
BOS	162	876	729	92	70
SEA	161	859	855	76	85
CHW	163	861	931	80	82
CLE	162	850	779	89	73
BAL	162	817	785	79	83
TOR	163	816	768	88	74
OAK	162	804	866	74	88
ANA	162	787	783	85	77
MIN	162	734	818	70	92
DET	162	722	863	65	97
KC	161	714	899	72	89
TB	162	620	751	63	99

(a) Calculate the marginal runs for each team, offensive and defensive. Because of interleague play, the runs and opponents runs will not be the same, so use runs as the basis.

(b) Give each team's projected winning percentage and number of wins based on marginal runs. How does this compare to the Pythgorean Number that you computed in question 1(b) of chapter 6?

Hard Sliders

Consult the Internet (http://www.baseball-reference.com/teams/NYM/1986.shtml) for the 1986 New York Mets statistics. Calculate the win shares for all the players using the short-form method outlined in the following steps:

a. Calculate runs created for all the hitters
b. Make the adjustment for marginal runs and determine offensive win shares
c. calculate pitching win shares for the team
d. Find the fielding win shares for all the non-pitchers
e. Calculate total win shares for each player.

For 1986 RC, use HDG23:

A = H + BB+ HBP − CS-GIDP
B = TB + [0.29(BB + HBP-IBB)] + [0.53(SF + SH)] + [0.64(SB)] − 0.03(K)
C = AB + BB + HBP + SH + SF

Split-Fingered Fastball

Adjust the total win shares computed in the "Hard Sliders" section to reflect 48 percent offense / 35 percent pitching / 17 percent defense, making sure that the total is exactly 3 × 108 = 324. Justify your alterations in essay form.

Seventh-Inning Stretch: Non-Sabermetrical Factors

Thus far we have considered a number of measures and instruments, such as linear weights, popularized by John Thorn and Pete Palmer, and runs created and win shares, as defined by Bill James. The computations are basically simple: we take whatever statistics are available, substitute them into a formula, and get a result, generally a number. Following this comes the interpretation of the number in light of many questions, such as:

- How does this statistic compare with other players?
- Is it a cumulative measure or an aggregate measure?
- Does this number change significantly during different eras with respect to comparable players of different eras?

But in baseball, especially from a sabermetrical point of view, things are not quite this simple. While in almost every sense the numbers add up, there were (and still are) other factors which affect the national pastime, many times in negative ways. Additionally, these factors are virtually impossible to quantify. Therefore, we are forced to take a more qualitative approach, framing these factors with some observations and with questions which can never be summarily answered. To name but three, these factors include: racial discrimination, economic escalation with respect to salaries, and a decade filled with speculations and accusations of steroid use and related factors dealing with physical enhancement.

It is primarily due to the existence of these non-sabermetrical factors that a sabermetrical argument does not and cannot provide us with the same degree of certainty as a mathematical proof. Yet these factors do provide much fodder for conversation whenever serious baseball fans gather.

Some non-sabermetrical factors to consider include:

- The color barrier
- Evolution of equipment and playing fields
- Technological and medical improvements
- League expansion
- Night baseball
- The Designated Hitter
- Interleague play
- Divisional play
- Wild cards
- Free agency
- The steroid controversy
- Changes in rules

Let's look at the last one, changes in rules, and let's consider how the home run has been affected. There was a time when present ground-rule doubles were counted as home runs; that is, batted balls which bounced into the stands were ruled to be home runs. On the other hand, baseballs which cleared the fence in fair territory, but curved around the foul pole and landing in the seats on the "foul" side (think of the Pesky Pole in Fenway Park) were called foul balls. To further muddy these waters, consider the following situation: say the score was tied 1–1 in the bottom of the ninth, with a runner on third base. If the batter hit the ball out of the park, he was given credit for only a single, the reason being that the winning run had scored from third needing just a single, thereby ending the game.

These are just examples of how non-sabermetrical factors (in this case, changes in rules) have affected home runs. It would be a statistical nightmare to try to go back and "fix" these totals. Perhaps in the long run, things balance out, perhaps not. In any event, there's not much that can be done. Babe Ruth will forever have 714 home runs. Not 713 or 715.

We now present ten random questions, realizing that many, many other questions could follow:

- Can one compare the fielding of Johnny Evers with that of Bill Mazeroski?
- Were the baseballs of 1901, 1920, 1930, 1968 and 2001 the same?
- Would Ty Cobb spike Jackie Robinson?
- Was Mark McGwire a better home run hitter than Mickey Mantle?
- What would the 1932 statistics of Jimmie Foxx have earned him in 2005?
- If the Designated Hitter rule was in effect in 1914, would Babe Ruth have remained a pitcher?
- What if Willie Mays had been a free agent in 1960?
- What numbers would have been recorded by Josh Gibson if he played for twenty seasons in the major leagues?

- Who threw the speediest fastball: Walter Johnson, Lefty Grove, Bob Feller or Nolan Ryan?
- Have Major League Baseball records been compromised of late?

Let's do some rambling. Both Evers and Mazeroski are in the Hall of Fame. Were the fields of 100 years ago as well kept as Forbes Field in 1960? What if Evers used Maz's glove and vice versa? Would the cleaner baseball of the 1960s be a help or hindrance for the infielder of a century ago? Would Maz have hit the Series-winning home run if Yankee hurler Ralph Terry had thrown a 1910 baseball?

You can surely think of several scenarios in which some of the factors listed above could have changed the game. Some of these factors are connected. For example, some batters now wear what amounts to body armor to protect their elbows from fastballs or ankles from foul balls. Helmets are lighter yet more protective. Equipment has evolved. One hundred years ago, players didn't have helmets or elbow pads. Pitchers still pitched inside, and players were still hit by pitches, but without the body armor, players either played hurt or they were placed on a disabled list. Now, oftentimes a pitcher is warned if he pitches inside. That's not a rule change, per se, but it is a non-sabermetrical factor that has affected the game.

When the duration of the regular season was lengthened from 154 to 162 games in 1961, Ford Frick was the Major League Baseball commissioner (he served as commissioner from 1951 to 1965, after having been the president of the National League from 1934 to 1951). He ruled that any records which surpassed those of the 154-game season but which also were made after 154 games (say, in the 161st game), would contain an asterisk. The most famous case was with Roger Maris and his chase of Babe Ruth's 60-homers-in-a-season record. Another example was Maury Wills' assault on the season stolen-base record of Ty Cobb (96). Wills heisted 104 bases in 1962. Frick would not budge on his decision to have two records, one with an asterisk. Eventually, the asterisk was struck from the record book; the point is now moot as several players have eclipsed the totals of Ruth and Maris, and of Cobb and Wills. However, as mentioned above, the asterisk gave players, fans, and sportswriters food for thought for decades.

A Hot-Stove League Question

List some other "non-sabermetrical" factors and specific questions.

A Fantasy League Question

You have just been named president of the National League for a day. Under the current agreement, when an interleague game is played in the National League city, the Designated Hitter is not used. Only players who field a position (including the pitcher) may bat. Conversely, in the American League city, the Designated Hitter is used and bats for the pitcher. One of the teams in the National League has a pitcher with a 10-game hitting streak. We're not sure what the record is (*The Sporting News Complete Baseball Record Book* does not contain this entry), but let's say it is ten games and you have a dilemma. If the pitcher pitches, does he take part in the game? If the Designated Hitter bats for him and goes 0 for 4, does the pitcher then lose his hitting streak? Do you advise the National League manager to bat the pitcher? Here are the offical rules from Major League Baseball:

Consecutive Hitting Streaks: A consecutive hitting streak shall not be terminated if the plate appearance results in a base on balls, hit batsman, defensive interference or a sacrifice bunt. A sacrifice fly shall terminate the streak.

Consecutive-Game Hitting Streaks: A consecutive-game hitting streak shall not be terminated if all the player's plate appearances (one or more) results in a base on balls, hit batsman, defensive interference or a sacrifice bunt. The streak shall terminate if the player has a sacrifice fly and no hit. The player's individual consecutive-game hitting streak shall be determined by the consecutive games in which the player appears and is not determined by his club's games.

Do any other non-sabermetrical factors come into play?

Inning 8: Park Effects

Regarding the effects of specific splaying fields, James again uses his axiomatic structure to describe outside influences on statistics. One of his "known principles of Sabermetrics" states, "Batting and pitching statistics never represent pure accomplishments, but are heavily colored by all kinds of illusions and extraneous effects. One of the most important of these is park effects." Anyone who has examined the numbers attained by players at Coors Field in recent years would certainly attest to that. But just how does one determine if a park favors hitters or pitchers?

Continuing the use of runs as the "currency," we can determine if a ballpark is more conducive to scoring runs or preventing them. A study of park factors provides an interesting look into how offensive statistics have changed over time as well. But what aspects of a ballpark contribute to its being designated "hitter friendly" or "pitcher friendly?"

The most obvious one is the distance of the fences from home plate, as that can seriously impact the number of home runs hit, or not hit. The last incarnation of the Polo Grounds in New York City, the home park of the Giants from 1912 to 1957, and for some time the Yankees as well, is considered a "pitchers' park." According to Phillip Lowry's wonderful publication *Green Cathedrals*, the distance from home plate to the left field wall was never more than 287 feet, and down the right field line was never more than 258. It seems that the Polo Grounds was a "hitters' park" as far as home runs were concerned, but a "pitchers' park" for other factors. The clubhouse steps in center field were 460 feet from the plate, thus giving the stadium a very distinctive horseshoe shape.

Other significant factors that play into a park's designation are the overall amount of foul territory, including the distance from home plate to the backstop. The Polo Grounds had what Lowry characterizes as a "huge" foul territory, with a distance from home plate to backstop listed variously from 65 to 74 feet.

But when we look at the effects of ballpark on the number of runs scored, we can get a clearer picture of how it should be viewed by computing the park factor. While there are different formulas for park factor, we will use the basic one:

$$\text{Park Factor} = \left(\frac{\left(\dfrac{\text{RunsScored(home)+RunsAllowed(home)}}{\text{Number of Home games}} \right)}{\left(\dfrac{\text{RunsScored(road)+RunsAllowed(road)}}{\text{Number of Road games}} \right)} \right).$$

Note that the numerator of the main fraction is the average of runs scored in the team's home games, while the denominator of the main fraction is the average of runs scored in the team's road games. Thus, if more runs are scored on average in the home games than in the road games, the fraction will have a value greater than 1, while if the average runs scored away from home is greater, the fraction will have a value less than 1. This can be figured as a percentage.

Obviously, any offensive statistic can be used in place of runs, provided one has the home/road splits for that statistic. In this way, a park's propensity for being favorable or unfavorable to that particular statistic can be quantified. Note also that a value of exactly 1 indicates a neutral effect on the statistic in question.

Since the expansion to 12 teams per league and the advent of divisional play in 1969, there were only three ballparks in the National League that were being used then and were still in use in 2006: the Cubs' Wrigley Field in Chicago, Dodger Stadium in Los Angeles, and the Mets' Shea Stadium in New York. We compare these three parks for runs production in those two seasons, 37 years apart. In 1969, the National League averaged 4.05 runs per team per game, while in 2006, the figure was 4.76. Both figures are off from the historic norm in major league baseball of 4.5 runs per team per game.

In 1969, the runs scored/runs allowed, home/road splits for the Cubs, Dodgers and Mets are:

	H-RS	H-RA	R-RS	R-RA
'69 CUBS	382	317	338	294
'69 LAD	325	258	320	303
'69 METS	308	266	324	275

Note that the "H" stands for home, "A" stands for away, "RS" for Runs Scored, and "RA" for Runs Allowed.

So, for the 1969 Cubs, the park factor for Wrigley Field is

$$\text{Park Factor} = \left(\frac{\left(\frac{\text{RunsScored(home)+RunsAllowed(home)}}{\text{Number of Home games}} \right)}{\left(\frac{\text{RunsScored(road)+RunsAllowed(road)}}{\text{Number of Road games}} \right)} \right)$$

$$= \left(\frac{\left(\frac{382+317}{81} \right)}{\left(\frac{338+294}{82} \right)} \right) = 1.11.$$

This can be interpreted that Wrigley Field increased run production by 11 percent over the course of the 1969 season.

Shea and Dodger Stadiums, respectively, have 1969 Park Factors of 0.96 and 0.94 (verify this using the data and the formula). This means Shea and Dodger decreased average run production by 4 percent and 6 percent respectively in 1969.

There is simplicity to this analysis. Often the average over a three-year period or a five-year period is used.

Consider the statistics for the first basemen of those teams that year, Wes Parker, Ernie Banks and Ed Kranepool:

Player	AB	H	2B	3B	HR	BB	SB	CS	TB	HBP	SH	SF	IBB	GIDP	K
Parker	471	131	23	4	13	56	4	1	201	2	6	6	6	10	46
Kranepool	353	84	9	2	11	49	3	2	130	0	2	4	7	10	32
Banks	565	143	19	2	23	42	0	0	235	7	8	7	7	15	101

Recall from chapter 6 that, for runs created version HDG-23,

A = H + BB + HBP − CS − GIDP

B = TB + [0.29 (BB + HBP − IBB)] + [0.53 (SF + SH)] + [0.64 (SB)] − 0.03(K)

C = AB + BB + HBP + SH + SF

and RC = $\dfrac{A \times B}{C}$.

Using HDG-23, the runs-created numbers for these players is 73.58 for Parker, 43.39 for Kranepool and 70.94 for Banks. Applying the park factors to these players' numbers, we consider that teams play half their games at home and half on the road, so we cut the park factor in half.

In this way, to compute park-adjusted runs created (PARC), we take RC + (1 − PF) × (RC)/2, so if a players' park factor is higher than 1, we will obtain a negative value for the (1 − PF) term, thus lowering his RC figure.

If he plays in a pitchers' park, his PF will be lower than 1, so (1 – PF) is a positive number, adjusting his RC upward.

Thus, if the home park for Banks increases run totals by 11 percent, his PARC is (70.94) + (1 – 1.11) × (70.94)/2 = 67.04. Parker's PARC is (73.58) + (1 – 0.94) × (73.58)/2 = 75.78, while Kranepool's is (43.39) + (1 – 0.96) × (43.39)/2 = 44.26.

Thirty-seven years later, Shea, Dodger and Wrigley have maintained more or less the same outfield dimensions. However, the degree to which each favored hitting or pitching changed slightly. Here are the home and road runs scored and allowed splits for the three teams in 2006:

	H-RS	H-RA	R-RS	R-RA
2006 CUBS	374	429	342	405
2006 LAD	438	365	382	386
2006 METS	395	347	439	384

The 2006 PF for Wrigley Field is

$$\text{Park Factor} = \left(\frac{\left(\dfrac{\text{RunsScored(home)}+\text{RunsAllowed(home)}}{\text{Number of Home games}} \right)}{\left(\dfrac{\text{RunsScored(road)}+\text{RunsAllowed(road)}}{\text{Number of Road games}} \right)} \right)$$

$$= \left(\frac{\left(\dfrac{374+429}{81} \right)}{\left(\dfrac{342+405}{82} \right)} \right) = 1.07.$$

It seems as though Wrigley was 4 percent less of a pitchers' park in 2006 then it was in 1969. What are some possible reasons for this? First, it may be that the number of hitters' parks league-wide had increased by 2006. In fact, there were 6 hitters' parks, 5 pitchers' parks and 1 neutral park in 1969, and in 2006 the totals were 8, 7 and 1, respectively. (You will be asked to verify these assertions in question 4 following this chapter.) However, in 1969, Wrigley Field was the number one hitters' park in the National League, but in 2006, it was 4th best, behind Cincinnati, Colorado, and Arizona.

What is even more interesting is the swing that occurred with Dodger Stadium. As stated earlier, Dodger Stadium could be seen as reducing run production by 6 percent, the second best pitchers' park in the National League, after Forbes Field in Pittsburgh. However, by 2006, it was the sixth-best hitters' park in the NL, with PF = 1.05 (verify this number). How could that be?

While the distances to the fences have not changed appreciably since 1969, according to *Green Cathedrals*, the backstop at Dodger Stadium was 75 feet from home plate in 1969 and 57 feet in 2006. Also, the foul territory was classified as large until 1999 and small since 2005. These factors also contribute to a park favoring a hitter.

It is better to use data from several years in order to determine PF. Very often, a three- or five-year average is used to dampen the effect of a team's particular strength or weakness in a particular season. Also, the home team's numbers are "washed out" in some versions of the formula, because home batters and pitchers do not face each other.

In 1992, the Baltimore Orioles opened Oriole Park at Camden Yards, which represented a renaissance in ballpark design. It combined modern amenities with a design that reminded people of such beloved bygone parks as Ebbets Field. Its success spawned many imitators, and while most of the stadiums built after Camden Yards seem to favor the hitter, Camden Yards has been pitcher-friendly throughout most of its history. In Table 10.1 we show the year-by-year park factors for Camden Yards since 1996, as there was a strike in 1994 and a shortened season in 1995.

PF	Season	H-RS	H-RA	R-RS	R-RA
0.892	1996	438	441	511	462
0.983	1997	389	351	423	330
0.894	1998	384	372	433	413
0.981	1999	419	406	432	409
0.897	2000	389	418	405	495
0.851	2001	305	392	382	437
0.957	2002	333	371	334	402
0.899	2003	362	373	381	447
1.077	2004	410	457	432	373
0.878	2005	330	385	399	415
0.985	2006	416	411	352	488

Table 10.1 The year-by-year totals, Oriole Park at Camden Yards, since 1996. (Note that the Orioles played 82 home games in 1996 and 82 road games in 2003.)

The 2004 season seems to stick out from all the others. Is it possible that a ballpark could depress runs totals by about 10 percent in one year and about 12 percent two years later, but inflate them by almost 8 percent in the year in between? Possible, sure. However, a check of *Green Cathedrals* turns up no significant alterations to Camden Yards for the 2003 season, making the sudden, temporary shift even less likely. Clearly, something is wrong with the formula. So, in an attempt to diminish the effect of one clearly anomalous season, we take a three-year average of PF. In other words, to establish a PF for a particular season, which we will call PF-3 (PF – 3 year average), we add up the PF for that season and the two previous ones, and divide by three, i.e.,

$$PF-3_{year} = \frac{(PF_{year} + PF_{year-1} + PF_{year-2})}{3}.$$

These can also be weighted further by games or innings. Thus, to establish a more accurate PF for a season, say 1999, we take

$$PF-3_{1999} = \frac{(PF_{1999} + PF_{1998} + PF_{1997})}{3}, \text{ or } PF-3_{1999} = \frac{(0.981 + 0.894 + 0.983)}{3} = 0.953.$$

The three-year averages are shown in Table 10.2

PF	Year	H-RS	H-RA	R-RS	R-RA	AVG
0.892	1996	438	441	511	462	—
0.983	1997	389	351	423	330	—
0.894	1998	384	372	433	413	0.923
0.981	1999	419	406	432	409	0.952
0.897	2000	389	418	405	495	0.924
0.851	2001	305	392	382	437	0.910
0.957	2002	333	371	334	402	0.901
0.899	2003	362	373	381	447	0.902
1.077	2004	410	457	432	373	0.977
0.878	2005	330	385	399	415	0.951
0.985	2006	416	411	352	488	0.980

Table 10.2 PF-3 calculations for Camden Yards since 1996.

Let us see how this can be applied to an individual player. Consider Melvin Mora, the Orioles' third baseman in 2003. Using HDG-23, Mora had a runs-created total of 133. However, his PARC = RC + (1 – PF) × (RC)/2 = 133 + (1 – 0.899) × (133)/2 = 140. If we consider the PF-3, then PARC-3 = RC + (1 – PF-3) × (RC)/2 = 133 + (1 – 0.902) × (133)/2 = 139. Despite this fine runs-created total, Mora placed only 18th in the American League Most Valuable Player balloting for 2004.

If we choose to average the PF over a half decade (and remember, this can be weighted by games and innings as well), we create PF-5. This provides even more stability than PF-3. Table 10.3 shows PF-5 calculations for Camden Yards between 1996 and 2006.

PF	Year	H-RS	H-RA	R-RS	R-RA	3-yr AVG	5-yr AVG
0.892	1996	438	441	511	462	—	—
0.983	1997	389	351	423	330	—	—
0.894	1998	384	372	433	413	0.923	—
0.981	1999	419	406	432	409	0.952	—
0.897	2000	389	418	405	495	0.924	0.929
0.851	2001	305	392	382	437	0.910	0.921
0.957	2002	333	371	334	402	0.901	0.916
0.899	2003	362	373	381	447	0.902	0.917
1.077	2004	410	457	432	373	0.977	0.936
0.878	2005	330	385	399	415	0.951	0.932
0.985	2006	416	411	352	488	0.980	0.959

Table 10.3 PF-5 calculations for Camden Yards since 1996

The park adjustments can shed even more light on the RC/27 statistic (see exercises, chapter 6). If we divide the runs-created total by the number $\frac{outs}{27}$, we obtain a figure that describes how many runs a team of 9 of a particular player might score per game. In 2003, Melvin Mora created 133 runs, using 382 outs to do it. Recall that outs are calculated by taking AB minus H and adding SH, SF and GIDP (but not CS) to that number. For 2004, Mora's unadjusted RC yields

$$RC/27 = \frac{133}{\frac{382}{27}} = 9.38,$$

while if we use PF the number is 9.02, and using PF-3 his RC/27 is 9.49. If we were to calculate his PF-5, we would see that his RC/27 would equal 9.68. This is an incredible range of difference in runs per game, and an indicator that, just maybe, Mora's season in 2004 did not receive the degree of recognition that it deserved.

Easy Tosses

1. Given the raw numbers for the left fielders for the Dodgers, Mets, and Cubs in 1969, (respectively, Willie Crawford, Cleon Jones and Billy Williams), compute and adjust their runs-created totals. Use HDG-23.

Player	AB	H	2B	3B	HR	BB	SB	CS	TB	HBP	SH	SF	IBB	GIDP	K	OUTS	PF
Crawford	389	96	17	5	11	49	4	5	156	0	2	0	3	5	85	300	0.94
Jones	483	164	25	4	12	64	16	8	233	7	1	3	10	11	60	334	0.96
Williams	642	188	33	10	21	59	3	2	304	59	0	3	15	15	70	472	1.11

2. (a) Use HDG-23 to compute the runs created for the 2006 third basemen on the Dodgers, Mets and Cubs (respectively, Aramis Ramirez,
David Wright, and Wilson Betamit).

Player	AB	H	2B	3B	HR	BB	SB	CS	TB	HBP	SH	SF	IBB	GIDP	K	OUTS
Betamit	174	42	7	0	9	17	1	0	76	0	0	2	3	7	45	141
Wright	582	181	40	5	26	66	20	5	309	5	0	8	13	15	113	424
A. Ramirez	594	173	38	4	38	50	2	1	333	9	0	7	4	15	63	443

(b) Apply PF from the chapter to adjust their RC numbers.

3. (a) Here are the runs scored and allowed splits for the Boston Red Sox
and the Oakland A's in 1969:

	H-RS	H-RA	R-RS	R-RA
'69 BOS	392	391	351	345
'69 OAK	330	315	410	363

Use the data to calculate the park factors for the teams that year.

(b) Here are the statistics for the left fielders for those respective clubs
in 1969:

Player	AB	H	2B	3B	HR	BB	SB	CS	TB	HBP	SH	SF	IBB	GIDP	K
Yastrzemski	603	154	28	2	40	101	15	7	306	1	0	2	9	14	91
Reynolds	315	81	10	0	2	34	1	3	97	8	4	2	1	8	29

Using HDG-23, calculate their runs-created total for 1969.

(c) Using the PF from part (a), adjust the runs-created totals of each
player in part (b), using the appropriate PF.

4. (a) Calculate the PF for each NL team in 1969. Classify each as
"Pitcher's," "Hitter's," or "Neutral."

Team	H-RS	H-RA	R-RS	R-RA
CIN	407	373	386	390
PIT	324	322	401	330
ChC	382	317	333	290

Team	H-RS	H-RA	R-RS	R-RA
SF	362	317	351	319
ATL	360	321	331	310
HOU	371	313	305	355
LaD	325	258	320	303
PHI	317	378	328	367
NYM	308	266	324	275
StL	276	276	318	264
MON	288	421	294	370
SD	239	358	229	388

(b) Repeat the directions for part (a) for the NL in 2006.

Team	H-RS	H-RA	R-RS	R-RA
PHI	444	420	421	392
ATL	414	390	435	415
NYM	395	347	439	384
LaD	438	365	382	386
COL	456	413	357	399
StL	404	352	382	414
ARI	403	429	370	359
FLA	353	371	405	401
SF	382	388	369	407
CIN	401	429	348	372
WAS	373	412	373	460
HOU	372	367	363	352
MIL	385	398	345	435
SD	315	337	416	342
ChC	374	429	342	405
PIT	380	367	311	430

5. (a) The ballpark in Oakland had a PF of 0.92 in 2006. It is historically a pitchers' park. Calculate the RC number for Nick Swisher using HDG-23.

	AB	H	2B	3B	HR	BB	SB	CS	TB	HBP	SH	SF	IBB	GIDP	K
N Swisher	556	141	24	2	35	97	1	2	274	11	2	6	7	13	152

(b) Calculate Swisher's RC/27, and adjust it for home park.

Hard Slider

1. (a) Calculate the PF for Fenway Park for each season from 1996 to 2003. Use the table below, and note that the Red Sox played 81 home games and only 80 road games in 2001. Are there any obvious anomalies?

Year	H-RS	H-RA	R-RS	R-RA
1996	517	464	411	457
1997	428	421	423	436
1998	439	364	437	365
1999	453	361	383	357
2000	394	380	398	365
2001	391	378	381	367
2002	396	353	463	312
2003	532	395	429	414

(b) Calculate PF-3 and PF-5 for each season where appropriate (see Baltimore calculations earlier in the chapter for guidance).

(c) Using HDG-23, calculate Manny Ramirez's Runs Created for the 2003 season.

Player	AB	H	2B	3B	HR	BB	SB	CS	TB	HBP	SH	SF	IBB	GIDP	K
MRamirez	569	185	36	1	37	97	3	1	334	8	0	5	8	28	94

(d) Adjust Ramirez's RC total using PF, PF-3, and PF-5, as calculated in part (b) .

(e) Calculate Manny's RC/27, and correct for home park.

(f) Were Manny Ramirez's runs created and RC/27 totals helped or hindered by Fenway Park? Justify your answer.

Inning 9: Creating Measures and Doing Sabermetrics — Some Examples

In their classic book *The Hidden Game of Baseball,* John Thorn and Pete Palmer write: "Baseball may be loved without statistics, but it cannot be understood without them." It seems that pretty much everyone associated with the game — from Henry Chadwick, who derived a "total bases per game" statistic circa 1860, to the present — agrees with Thorn and Palmer. Indeed the very purpose of this book is an attempt to better explain the game of baseball by using statistics.

In this book we have referred to Thorn and Palmer (and their linear weights), and others, such as Bill James (runs created), who have created well-known measures and instruments. As we have seen, each measure has certain properties and nuances.

There is an art to creating a measure: it should be fairly easy to understand and not too difficult to compute. For example, to compute a batting average (BA), one merely divides the total number of hits by the total number of at-bats. Rounded off to the nearest thousandth, it is not only easily computed but is also easily understood. The constituent *ingredients* of hits and at-bats are very easy to obtain from the sports section of newspapers, from baseball books, and from the Internet.

Continuing with this example, we see that the extremes range from .000 (no hits) to 1.000 (a hit every time one bats). Another property of this model is that *extra base hits* are weighted the same as singles. Also, this statistic gives no information about either runs batted in or runs scored. Nor does it reveal anything about streaks, clutch hitting (however we wish to define these two ideas), day vs. night performances, etc.

One way of dealing with some of the shortcomings of BA, is to use split statistics. Nowadays these numbers are easily found on the Web. Here, we can discover how well or poorly a batter does regarding such factors as: day vs. night, righty vs. lefty, natural grass vs. artificial turf, etc.

Batting averages can sometimes assist us in attempts to span eras. Players like Ty Cobb and Rogers Hornsby more than once batted over .400, yet no once since Ted Williams in 1941 has repeated this feat. And in 1968, Carl Yastrzemski led the American League with a mark of .301. Can these numbers be compared in any reasonable way?

One approach is to compare a player with his peers. For example, let us compare two batting champions. In 1911, Ty Cobb hit .420 while the league averaged .273; in 1968, the year Yastrzemski batted .301, the American league batted .230. If we divide Cobb's average by the league's mark we get a ratio of 1,538; repeating the process for Yastrzemski gives us 1.309. What do these numbers mean?

We can think of these ratios as normalization factors which may give us a sense of how these Hall of Famers performed relative to their peers. In other words, while there was a difference of 119 percentage points between the Georgia Peach and Yaz with respect to BA, we can think of Cobb as being 1.538 times as good as the 1911 average hitter in the American League, while his counterpart was 1.309 times as good as his peers.

It would seem that this approach does indeed shed new light on the "search for objective knowledge" about baseball. In particular, this methodology can assist us in leveling the playing fields when comparing players of different times. Bottom line: at times, ratios are more revealing than differences.

One final comment: there are many statistics which deal with hitting and quite a few which evaluate pitching. Because fielding is much more difficult to "measure," there are relatively few instruments dealing with this aspect of the game.

Here are some questions toward a methodology to assist in creating sabermetrical measures:

• What do I want the model to demonstrate?
• Does this instrument reveal something heretofore unknown?
• Does the model lend itself to clear interpretations?
• Can I easily obtain the constituent factors necessary for the model?
• Is the measure too difficult to compute, thereby rendering it virtually useless?
• Are there extreme cases? If so, what happens to the measure in these cases?
• What are the shortcomings of the instrument?

- Can I use the model for different eras?
- Do results from this model seem to agree with findings from the use of similar models?

Let's compare apples and oranges. Ty Cobb won 12 batting titles in 13 years (1907 through 1919, excepting 1916) while Babe Ruth gathered 13 slugging titles in 14 years (1918 through 1931, save 1925). It would be difficult to find two more dominant streaks in baseball history. Is there any instrument we can use to compare these two sustained performances?

As we know, batting averages range from .000 to 1.000, while slugging percentages can vary from .000 to 4.000. So differences between champions is not a realistic measure. For example, Cobb outhit the American League runner-up by 12 points in 1911 (.420 to .408) while Ruth outslugged his nearest rival by 215 points in 1920 (.847 to .632).

The league batting average in 1911 was .273; dividing this into Cobb's .420 mark gives a ratio of 1.538. We could interpret this as saying that Cobb was better that one and a half times the average league hitter in 1911. That's pretty impressive.

In 1920, the American League slugged .387. When this average is divided into Ruth's .847, we see arrive at a ratio of 2.189, perhaps interpreting this as saying that Ruth was better than twice the average slugger in 1920.

What does this mean? We're not sure; but when one "does the math" we find that Ruth's lowest ratio of the 13 years he won the title occurred in 1922, when he slugged .672, the league slugged .398, thus giving a ratio of 1.688. Cobb's *highest* ratio of 1.584 was compiled in 1910 when the league batted .243 and the Georgia Peach hit .385.

Was Ruth a better slugger than Cobb was a hitter? Maybe we can compare apples and oranges.

As mentioned above (and in Inning 7), it is extremely difficult to compare players from different eras. We can attempt to use normalization and relativity arguments. We have just used a hitting example, so now we try something in pitching.

Hugh Ignatius "One Arm" Daily played his first professional game for the Buffalo Bisons in 1882 at the age of 34. He would play baseball for six seasons, primarily as a pitcher, spending each season with a different team (Buffalo in 1882, the Cleveland Blues in 1883, Chicago/Pittsburgh and then the Washington Nationals in the Union League in 1884, the St. Louis Maroons of the NL in 1885, the Nationals again in 1886, and the Blues again in 1887. His career record was 73–87. So what? In 1884, he struck out 483 batters in 500⅔ innings pitched, enroute to a 28–28 record. This strikeout total ranks third all-time for a season. His single-season strikeouts-per-nine-innings-pitched (K/9IP) ratio was 8.682. This mark stood for 71 years, until Herb Score came along in 1955. That year, Score was voted Rookie of the Year with the Cleveland Indians, and he struck out 245 batters in 227⅓ innings (K/9IP = 9.699), sporting a 16–10 record. Score's achievement only lasted until 1960, when the Los Angeles Dodgers' Sandy Koufax struck out 197 men in 175 innings, giving him a K/9IP of 10.131. Koufax broke his own record in 1962 (remember, after league expansion), with 216 K in 184⅓ innings (K/9IP = 10.546), and he finished that season with a 14–7 showing. The record came back to Cleveland when Sudden Sam McDowell set a new mark of K/9IP = 10.714 (325 K in 273 IP) in 1965; McDowell's feat stood until 1984 when another Rookie of the Year, the Mets' Dwight "Doc" Gooden, notched 276 K in 218 IP (K/9IP = 11.394). Nolan Ryan bested that three years later, posting K/9IP = 11.480 (270 / 211⅔), at the age of 40, going 8–16 for the Houston Astros. Seattle's Randy Johnson broke the 12 K/9IP level, the Cubs' Kerry Wood (in his 1998 Rookie of the Year season) beat Johnson, Boston's Pedro Martinez topped 13 K/9IP in 1999, and Randy Johnson again set a new record of 13.410 K/9IP (372 strikeouts in 249⅔ innings) in a season in which he won 21 games and was named World Series Most Valuable Player.

How can we rate the significance of each pitcher? Hugh Daily's 483 strikeouts will probably never be bested. Some of the pitchers on the list had dismal win-loss records yet managed to have a high frequency of strikeouts when they were in a game. By 1903, Rube Waddell had the career mark of just over 7 strikeouts per 9 innings. Bob Feller overtook him for a while but then tailed off toward the end of his career, giving the record back to Waddell. Sandy Koufax and Nolan Ryan also held the career ratio record until Randy Johnson grabbed it in 1994, and Johnson has held it ever since. The Big Unit's career mark was as high as 11.207 in 2002 but had dropped to 10.776 at the end of the 2006 season.

Are we comparing apples to oranges in this case? Should we bring in the normalization factor and compare each of the single-season marks to the league average? Probably so, as the only pitchers to record more than 350 strikeouts in a single season who did *not* pitch in the 1800s are Sandy Koufax (1965), Nolan Ryan (1973 and 1974) and Randy Johnson (1999 and 2001). Interestingly, Koufax pitched 335⅔ innings in 1965; that's when Sam McDowell set the K/9IP record.

Is anyone interested in strikeouts per nine innings pitched? Sure. However, one of the questions we must ask is does the instrument reveal something? What are the shortcomings of trying to compare players from vastly different eras with this statistic? Should we try to use it for different eras? Since expansion in the mid–1990s, many experts feel that offense has taken over the game of baseball. Home runs are flying out of the park. The ball is juiced. Pitching is diluted. Perhaps a significant pitching statistic, such as K/9IP, which shows improvement in recent years, will give those experts something else to ponder.

Now, it's time for a few examples of using sabermetrics. We will discuss examples of using measures to study batting, pitching, fielding, and team performance. First, let's talk about hitting.

If we know a player's batting average and slugging average, we can use a new statistic called Isolated Power (ISO), which was an outgrowth of studies done by Branch Rickey and Allen Roth in the 1940s and 1950s. Its formula is ISO = SLG – BA and it essentially takes the singles out of a player's batting average to measure power hitting. Since first base is often a source of power in a team's lineup, let's apply the statistic there. Say, for example, we wanted to determine which was the better offensive first baseman from the past, Hall of Famer George Sisler of the St. Louis Browns or Brooklyn Dodger Gil Hodges. Sisler had a career BA of .340 (2812 H / 8267 AB), one of the top 15 of all time, and a career SLG of .468. Gil Hodges, on the other hand, had a career BA of .273 (1921 H / 7030 AB) and career SLG of .487 (3422 TB / 7030 AB). While Sisler's raw numbers seems superior, their ISO numbers tell a different story. His ISO is .128, while Hodges' is .214. Now wait a minute, you might argue. Isn't Sisler is being penalized for having such a lofty career average? After all, he outslugged and outhit Hodges. That may be a valid point. So, when we look at their respective OPS and SLOB, the result is at least mildly surprising. Hodges had an OBA of .359, while Sisler had a .376. Thus, their respective OPS and SLOB are .176 and .844 for Sisler and .175 and .844 for Hodges, numbers that indicate that it's a dead heat.

How does Greg Maddux stack up against the greatest pitchers of all time? Consider the following statistical lines for Maddux and Hall of Famer Sandy Koufax:

	G	GS	W	L	IP	ER	SO	BB	H	ShO	ERA
Koufax, '64	29	28	19	5	223	43	223	53	154	7	1.74
Maddux, '94	25	25	16	6	202	35	156	31	150	3	1.56

The years seem pretty equal, but Koufax had more innings pitched and more strikeouts, and Maddux was 20 points better in Earned Run Average. How can you compare two pitchers that faced different batters in different eras?

In 1964, the National League's aggregate ERA was 3.54. If one were to divide the league ERA by Koufax's, we obtain a statistic that sabermetrician Pete Palmer termed the relative ERA. Koufax's relative ERA for 1964 was 3.54 / 1.74 = 2.03, indicating that Koufax was about twice as good as the average pitcher that year. Maddux's 1994 ERA of 1.56 was attained in a season that the National League's ERA was 4.21, making his Relative ERA 4.21 / 1.56 = 2.70. By this measure, one could make the argument that Maddux's season was significantly better than that of Koufax.

One of the most difficult aspects of baseball to quantify is defense. While Fielding Percentage had long been the standard by which defense was calibrated, James introduced a statistic called range factor which gives additional insight. Consider the 1955 season; New York Giant immortal Willie Mays played 152 games and had 407 outfield putouts, 23 assists and made 8 errors. His fielding percentage, (PO + AS) / (PO + AS + E) = .982. Larry Doby, then of the Chicago White Sox, played 129 games and had 313 putouts, 6 assists and 2 errors, for a fielding percentage of .994. Doby might have been judged the better fielder; however, range factor, which measures successful chances per game (ignoring errors), favors Mays. His range factor in 1955 was (PO + AS) / G, or (407 + 23) / 152 = 2.83, while Doby's was (313 + 6) / 129 = 2.47. The difference in their Range Factors was .36, which may not seem like much, but translates to 36 more successful chances in just 100 games.

Sabermetrician and noted author Rob Neyer has used the standard deviation to create a statistic called the SD score. It is a measure of how far a team's runs scored and allowed relate to the league average. It is the sum of the number of standard deviations above the league's mean in runs scored plus the number of standard deviations below the mean in runs allowed. History shows that excellent teams are associated with an SD score above three, average teams score around zero, and poor teams score in the negative numbers. The 1998 New York Yankees had an SD score of 3.81, the best in the 20th century.

The following chart gives the SD scores for the American League in 2002. Using this method, one is less surprised by the World Series victory by the wild card Anaheim Angels. The Oakland Athletics' early playoff exit is also less surprising, and the managerial effort of Minnesota's Ron Gardenhire can be better appreciated.

AL2002	SD Score	W	L	PCT
Anaheim	2.279	99	63	0.611
New York	2.202	103	58	0.640
Boston	2.136	93	69	0.574

AL2002	SD Score	W	L	PCT
Oakland	1.608	103	59	0.636
Seattle	1.266	93	69	0.574
Chicago	0.639	81	81	0.500
Minnesota	0.617	94	67	0.584
Toronto	-0.17	78	84	0.481
Texas	-0.43	72	90	0.444
Cleveland	-1.08	74	88	0.457
Baltimore	-1.17	67	95	0.414
Kansas City	-1.7	62	100	0.383
Tampa Bay	-2.7	55	106	0.342
Detroit	-3.18	55	106	0.342

Powerful Quests

1. Consider all players with at least 500 lifetime home runs. Define the cumulative home run ratio (CHR) as the number of home runs (HR) divided by the number of at-bats (AB) leading up to a particular age. (For example, if Player X hit 5 HR in 100 AB at the age of 20, his CHR = 5/100 = .050. If he hit 10 HR in 100 AB at the age of 21, his CHR now increases to: (5+10)/(100+100) = .075). Compare each player's CHR with his age for their entire careers.

2. Ken Riordan of Inverness, Florida, has developed a measure he calls the peer ratio. With this instrument, Riordan computes a statistic, say the major league slugging percentage over the span of a particular player's career, and divides this number into the corresponding career statistic of the player to get his peer ratio. For example, Ted Williams had a slugging average of .634 over a career that spanned from 1939 through 1960. Over the same period, major league batters slugged .381, giving Williams a peer ratio of .634/.391 = 1.664. Discuss the pros and cons of this measure.

Swing and a Miss

1. No-hitters have declined in recent years. One of the factors may be the low number of innings that starters pitch. Roy Halliday led the American League with only five complete games in 2005. Compare five pitchers from

each league who have had at least 200 innings pitched in the last three seasons. What was the average number of innings per start? What was the average number of hits per inning pitched? Now look at a few of the pitchers who have thrown no-hitters in the past (Nolan Ryan, Sandy Koufax, etc.). What was their ratio of hits per nine innings? Innings per start? What conclusions (if any) can you draw?

Easy Tosses

1. Refer back to Inning 4, "Hard Sliders" Problem 3. Which of the six doubles leaders has the highest ISO?

2. In 1968, St. Louis Cardinals ace Bob Gibson posted an ERA of 1.12, causing Major League Baseball to lower the height on the mound the following season. That was the only season in which Gibson led the league in ERA. In 2005, Roger Clemens led the league for the 7th time in ERA, posting a mark of 1.87. Compare their relative ERAs.

3. Cleon Jones and Paul Blair were both signed by the New York Mets in the amateur drafts of 1963 and 1962, respectively. They played against each other in the 1969 World Series, Blair in the Baltimore Orioles outfield and Jones in the Mets outfield. Compare their range factors and fielding percentages. Use a relative argument.

Extra Innings:
Beyond Sabermetrics

Those who practice sabermetrics are searching for objective truth in baseball. They try to determine who the best players were (and are), by developing formulae that compare and contrast players. They have looked at the simple statistics of the first 100 years of major league baseball and tried to create well-accepted measures, starting with batting average and earned run average, and then moving to runs created, linear weights, and win shares, to support their claims. Can we develop predictions and rankings of players and teams with sabermetrical analyses alone? Several major league baseball teams are now using full-time professional statistical analysts to find patterns to provide valuable information to managers. Managers then can decide whether to use this statistical information in making decisions during a game. There are a host of sabermetrical websites, including mlb.com, which provide data and trends directly to the ballclubs. Baseball statisticians have popularized the notion that it is possible to answer a variety of questions about the game by means of statistical analyses. In this chapter we go beyond the accepted stats and ponder more rigorous statistical analyses. We will develop the ideas behind simulation and regression, useful tools in developing measures to analyze complicated data.

Simulation

As a first example, let's consider that in 1941, Joe DiMaggio was 26 years old and already a star on the New York Yankees. The Yankees had won the World Series in each of DiMaggio's first four seasons, 1936 through 1939, but were coming off of a third-place finish in 1940. DiMaggio had won the Most Valuable Player Award in 1939, and he had finished third in the MVP voting in 1940, behind Hank Greenberg and Bob Feller. He had been named to the American League All-Star Team in each of his first five seasons. In 1940, DiMaggio was the club leader in batting average, on-base percentage, slugging percentage (and therefore in OPS), hits, total bases, home runs, runs batted in, singles, adjusted OPS+, runs created, at-bats per strikeout, and at-bats per home run. It was good to be Joltin' Joe DiMaggio, the Yankee Clipper. Could it get any better?

As you already know, 1941 became the year that Joe DiMaggio established the one record that will probably never be broken. He hit safely in 56 consecutive games, breaking Wee Willie Keeler's mark of 44 straight games, set in 1897. DiMaggio became only the third player in the twentieth century to hit safely in at least 40 consecutive games (the others being Ty Cobb with 40 in 1911, and George Sisler with 41 in 1922) Pete Rose in 1978 would become the only other player to hit in at least 40 straight games.

Never be broken, you ask? How can we be sure? Let's go beyond the sabermetrics and create a simulation of Joe DiMaggio's 1941 season. Several researchers have investigated DiMaggio's hitting streak, creating complicated simulations and resolving probabilities in a game-to-game fashion. We seek to simulate a hitting streak in a simple yet reliable manner. Let's develop the tools necessary to recreate the opportunity that Joe had. First, in order to create an effective simulation, we look at the actual data from 1941.

| | | | | | | | Batting Line | | | |
Game	Date	Pitcher(s)	Team	AB	R	H	2B	3B	HR	RBI
1	5/15/1941	Eddie Smith	Chicago	4	0	1	0	0	0	1
2	5/16/1941	Thornton Lee	Chicago	4	2	2	0	1	1	1
3	5/17/1941	Johnny Rigney	Chicago	3	1	1	0	0	0	0
4	5/18/1941	Bob Harris	St. Louis			2				
		Johnny Niggeling		3	3		1	0	0	1
5	5/19/1941	Denny Galehouse	St. Louis	3	0	1	1	0	0	0
6	5/20/1941	Elden Auker	St. Louis	5	1	1	0	0	0	1
7	5/21/1941	Schoolboy Rowe	Detroit			1				
		Al Benton		5	0	1	0	0	0	1
8	5/22/1941	Archie McKain	Detroit	4	0	1	0	0	0	1
9	5/23/1941	Dick Newsome	Boston	5	0	1	0	0	0	2
10	5/24/1941	Earl Johnson	Boston	4	2	1	0	0	0	2
11	5/25/1941	Lefty Grove	Boston	4	0	1	0	0	0	0

Game	Date	Pitcher(s)	Team	AB	R	Batting Line H	2B	3B	HR	RBI
12	5/27/1941	Ken Chase	Washington			1				
		Red Anderson				2				
		Alex Carrasquel		5	3	1	0	0	1	3
13	5/28/1941	Sid Hudson	Washington	4	1	1	0	1	0	0
14	5/29/1941	Steve Sundra	Washington	3	1	1	0	0	0	0
15	5/30/1941	Earl Johnson	Boston	2	1	1	0	0	0	0
16	5/30/1941	Mickey Harris	Boston	3	0	1	1	0	0	0
17	6/1/1941	Al Milnar	Cleveland	4	1	1	0	0	0	0
18	6/1/1941	Mel Harder	Cleveland	4	0	1	0	0	0	0
19	6/2/1941	Bob Feller	Cleveland	4	2	2	1	0	0	0
20	6/3/1941	Dizzy Trout	Detroit	4	1	1	0	0	1	1
21	6/5/1941	Hal Newhouser	Detroit	5	1	1	0	1	0	1
22	6/7/1941	Bob Muncrief	St. Louis			1				
		Johnny Allen				1				
		George Caster		5	2	1	0	0	0	1
23	6/8/1941	Elden Auker	St. Louis	4	3	2	0	0	2	4
24	6/8/1941	George Caster	St. Louis			1				
		Jack Kramer		4	1	1	1	0	1	3
25	6/10/1941	Johnny Rigney	Chicago	5	1	1	0	0	0	0
26	6/12/1941	Thornton Lee	Chicago	4	1	2	0	0	1	1
27	6/14/1941	Bob Feller	Cleveland	2	0	1	1	0	0	1
28	6/15/1941	Jim Bagby	Cleveland	3	1	1	0	0	1	1
29	6/16/1941	Al Milnar	Cleveland	5	0	1	1	0	0	0
30	6/17/1941	Johnny Rigney	Chicago	4	1	1	0	0	0	0
31	6/18/1941	Thornton Lee	Chicago	3	0	1	0	0	0	0
32	6/19/1941	Eddie Smith	Chicago			1				
		Buck Ross		3	2	2	0	0	1	2
33	6/20/1941	Bobo Newsom	Detroit			2				
		Archie McKain		5	3	2	1	0	0	1
34	6/21/1941	Dizzy Trout	Detroit	4	0	1	0	0	0	1

Game	Date	Pitcher(s)	Team	AB	R	Batting Line H	2B	3B	HR	RBI
35	6/22/1941	Hal Newhouser	Detroit			1				
		Bobo Newsom		5	1	1	1	0	1	2
36	6/24/1941	Bob Muncrief	St. Louis	4	1	1	0	0	0	0
37	6/25/1941	Denny Galehouse	St. Louis	4	1	1	0	0	1	3
38	6/26/1941	Elden Auker	St. Louis	4	0	1	1	0	0	1
39	6/27/1941	Chubby Dean	Philadelphia	3	1	2	0	0	1	2
40	6/28/1941	Johnny Babich	Philadelphia			1				
		Lum Harris		5	1	1	1	0	0	0
41	6/29/1941	Dutch Leonard	Washington	4	1	1	1	0	0	0
42	6/29/1941	Red Anderson	Washington	5	1	1	0	0	0	1
43	7/1/1941	Mickey Harris	Boston			1				
		Mike Ryba		4	0	1	0	0	0	1
44	7/1/1941	Jack Wilson	Boston	3	1	1	0	0	0	1
45	7/2/1941	Dick Newsome	Boston	5	1	1	0	0	1	3
46	7/5/1941	Phil Marchildon	Philadelphia	4	2	1	0	0	1	2
47	7/6/1941	Johnny Babich	Philadelphia			2				
		Bump Hadley		5	2	2	1	0	0	2
48	7/6/1941	Jack Knott	Philadelphia	4	0	2	0	1	0	2
49	7/10/1941	Johnny Niggeling	St. Louis	2	0	1	0	0	0	0
50	7/11/1941	Bob Harris	St. Louis			3				
		Jack Kramer		5	1	1	0	0	1	2
51	7/12/1941	Elden Auker	St. Louis			1				
		Bob Muncrief		5	1	1	1	0	0	1
52	7/13/1941	Ted Lyons	Chicago			2				
		Jack Hallett		4	2	1	0	0	0	0
53	7/13/1941	Thornton Lee	Chicago	4	0	1	0	0	0	0
54	7/14/1941	Johnny Rigney	Chicago	3	0	1	0	0	0	0
55	7/15/1941	Eddie Smith	Chicago	4	1	2	1	0	0	2
56	7/16/1941	Al Milnar	Cleveland			2				
		Joe Krakauskas		4	3	1	1	0	0	0
TOTALS				223	56	91	16	4	15	55

From this data, we'll develop a table of outcomes from the hitting streak. For example, we notice that Joe had at least two at-bats in every game of the streak. The most at-bats in a single game was five. Therefore, we create a table showing the distribution of at-bats in the 56 games. Table 12.1 shows this distribution. In the first column are the number of possible at-bats. In the next column are the observed values for each amount of at-bats. Next is the percentage of that number of at-bats occurring (the count divided by 56, the total number of games in the streak). The last column shows the cumulative percentage for up to six at-bats in a single game.

AB	Count	%	Cum %
0	0	0.00%	0.00%
1	0	0.00%	0.00%
2	3	5.36%	5.36%
3	11	19.64%	25.00%
4	26	46.43%	71.43%
5	16	28.57%	100.00%
6	0	0.00%	100.00%
TOTAL	56	100.00%	100.00%

Table 12.1 Distribution of at-bat occurrences

Table 12.1 shows us that Joe had 11 out of 56 games in which he had three official at-bats, or he had three at-bats in 19.64 percent of the games during the streak. Further, he had *no more than* three at-bats in 25 percent of the 56 games. In a simulation of the streak, we would expect him to have similar percentages of games with three or fewer at-bats. We note a few things here. Is it possible to have no at-bats, or just one at-bat in a game? Rule 10.24 of the *Major League Baseball Official Rule Book* provides the following guidelines for cumulative hitting streaks:

First, "a consecutive hitting streak shall not be terminated if the plate appearance results in a base on balls, hit batsman, defensive interference or a sacrifice bunt. A sacrifice fly shall terminate the streak." This means that if Joe had no official at-bats in a game (for example, he walked in four plate appearances), the streak would continue.

Second, "a consecutive game hitting streak shall not be terminated if all the player's plate appearances (one or more) result in a base on balls, hit batsman, defensive interference or a sacrifice bunt. The streak shall terminate if the player has a sacrifice fly and no hit. The player's individual consecutive game hitting streak shall be determined by the consecutive games in which the player appears and is not determined by his club's games." This is very similar to the first guideline from the *Official Rule Book*, except it points out that a hitting streak remains intact if the player sits out a game, even though the team plays.

How does this affect the probabilities? The probability of getting no at-bats during a hitting streak is zero. Even though Joe had no games with only one at-bat, the probability exists that it could occur, so in the simulation, we will designate a probability (albeit a small one); we fix the probability of one at-bat in a game to be 0.10 percent. Similarly, although Joe did not have any six-at-bat games, we will fix the probability at 0.10 percent that it could occur. We will not expect any single games with at-bats greater than six. Table 12.2 shows the adjusted table of probabilities. The last column is just a decimal representation of the percentage.

AB	Adjusted %	Cum %	Number
0	0.00%	0.00%	0.000
1	0.10%	0.10%	0.001
2	5.36%	5.46%	0.055
3	19.64%	25.10%	0.251
4	46.43%	71.53%	0.715
5	28.37%	99.90%	0.999
6	0.10%	100.00%	1.000
TOTAL	100.00%	100.00%	1.000

Table 12.2 **Distribution of adjusted at-bat percentages**

Now we are ready to begin the simulation. Using a spreadsheet program (such as Microsoft Excel), we will generate random numbers. We need to determine the number of official at-bats per game and then determine whether or not each at-bat results in a hit or in an out. Take a look at Figure 12.1. This shows a screen capture of one such simulation.

In the upper left we designate a batting average (shown in cell D2) of 0.333. Our screen capture has a "slider bar" to adjust the batting average, but that is not necessary. This simulation will model a 162-game season. Column B in the spreadsheet shows the game number. In column C, we generate a random number, which will determine the number of at-bats in the game. For example, the computer generated 0.233 (cell C8 in Figure 13.1). Looking at the right-most column of Table 13.2, we see that 0.233 falls between 0.055 and 0.251 (the chance of 2 and 3 at-bats). Therefore, we set the at-bat value at 3 (see cell D8), using a conditional formatting command. Since the random number generated in cell C9 is 0.357 (between 0.251 and 0.715), the number of at-bats is 4 (cell D9). This process is repeated for all

Batting Average = 0.333   ◄ ▣ ▦ ►   Max Streak = 21 | 0.000 | H |
                                                          | 0.333 | Out |

Simulated Season BA = 0.355

Game	Random # for AB	AB	Random # for Hit in each AB						1	2	3	4	5	6	H	Streak
1	0.233	3	0.592	0.491	0.906	0.057	0.424	0.976	Out	Out	Out				0	0
2	0.357	4	0.404	0.426	0.714	0.342	0.983	0.592	Out	Out	Out	Out			0	0
3	0.186	3	0.899	0.627	0.852	0.922	0.316	0.663	Out	Out	Out				0	0
4	0.725	5	0.875	0.947	0.574	0.130	0.619	0.137	Out	Out	Out	Hit	Out		1	1
5	0.331	4	0.172	0.441	0.915	0.222	0.933	0.032	Hit	Out	Out	Hit			2	2
6	0.976	5	0.522	0.901	0.934	0.214	0.704	0.739	Out	Out	Out	Hit	Out		1	3
7	0.515	4	0.821	0.426	0.307	0.786	0.250	0.776	Out	Out	Hit	Out			1	4
8	0.514	4	0.357	0.829	0.425	0.646	0.741	0.375	Out	Out	Out	Out			0	0
9	0.321	4	0.650	0.370	0.130	0.721	0.121	0.922	Out	Out	Hit	Out			1	1
10	0.345	4	0.269	0.480	0.737	0.990	0.594	0.979	Hit	Out	Out	Out			1	2
11	0.363	4	0.738	0.923	0.651	0.947	0.545	0.504	Out	Out	Out	Out			0	0
12	0.887	5	0.655	0.211	0.146	0.598	0.332	0.104	Out	Hit	Hit	Out	Hit		3	1
13	0.344	4	0.768	0.295	0.914	0.229	0.461	0.057	Out	Hit	Out	Hit			2	2
14	0.082	3	0.033	0.591	0.540	0.602	0.203	0.940	Hit	Out	Out				1	3
15	0.547	4	0.101	0.505	0.201	0.970	0.208	0.430	Hit	Out	Hit	Out			2	4
16	0.796	5	0.011	0.709	0.642	0.755	0.175	0.784	Hit	Out	Out	Out	Hit		2	5
17	0.231	3	0.451	0.605	0.980	0.192	0.406	0.490	Out	Out	Out				0	0
18	0.495	4	0.154	0.221	0.756	0.453	0.822	0.065	Hit	Hit	Out	Out			2	1
19	0.374	4	0.907	0.454	0.783	0.422	0.410	0.426	Out	Out	Out	Out			0	0
20	0.269	4	0.843	0.064	0.305	0.572	0.642	0.370	Out	Hit	Hit	Out			2	1
21	0.404	4	0.391	0.496	0.059	0.995	0.729	0.580	Out	Out	Hit	Out			1	2
22	0.887	5	0.018	0.681	0.647	0.058	0.357	0.584	Hit	Out	Out	Hit	Out		2	3
23	0.839	5	0.711	0.105	0.028	0.072	0.619	0.085	Out	Hit	Hit	Hit	Out		3	4
24	0.651	4	0.948	0.643	0.017	0.496	0.287	0.884	Out	Out	Hit	Out			1	5
25	0.311	4	0.047	0.785	0.378	0.643	0.313	0.519	Hit	Out	Out	Out			1	6
26	0.943	5	0.035	0.171	0.760	0.019	0.129	0.118	Hit	Hit	Out	Hit	Hit		4	7
27	0.552	4	0.499	0.037	0.630	0.540	0.056	0.496	Out	Hit	Out	Out			1	8
28	0.754	5	0.184	0.837	0.916	0.440	0.390	0.593	Hit	Out	Out	Out	Out		1	9
29	0.302	4	0.067	0.005	0.394	0.849	0.082	0.021	Hit	Hit	Out	Out			2	10
30	0.798	5	0.324	0.731	0.939	0.024	0.989	0.734	Hit	Out	Out	Hit	Out		2	11
31	0.338	4	0.196	0.927	0.891	0.094	0.562	0.744	Hit	Out	Out	Hit			2	12
32	0.773	5	0.914	0.334	0.863	0.616	0.080	0.519	Out	Out	Out	Out	Hit		1	13
33	0.392	4	0.041	0.559	0.040	0.920	0.587	0.879	Hit	Out	Hit	Out			2	14
34	0.608	4	0.175	0.412	0.064	0.562	0.610	0.486	Hit	Out	Hit	Out			2	15
35	0.865	5	0.819	0.881	0.918	0.110	0.161	0.262	Out	Out	Out	Hit	Hit		2	16
36	0.726	5	0.008	0.449	0.636	0.041	0.187	0.454	Hit	Out	Out	Hit	Hit		3	17
37	0.708	4	0.944	0.852	0.101	0.501	0.469	0.977	Out	Out	Hit	Out			1	18
38	0.952	5	0.424	0.396	0.946	0.446	0.026	0.155	Out	Out	Out	Out	Hit		1	19
39	0.575	4	0.645	0.313	0.784	0.385	0.546	0.080	Out	Hit	Out	Out			1	20
40	0.155	4	0.822	0.180	0.343	0.891	0.328	0.710	Out	Hit	Out	Out			1	21
41	0.266	4	0.758	0.423	0.788	0.995	0.888	0.150	Out	Out	Out	Out			0	0

Figure 12.1 A simulation of a hitting streak

162 games. Next we generate six random numbers for each possible at-bat (columns E through J). The output of each number will be displayed in columns K through P. Depending on the value of cell D8, only those columns corresponding to the number of at-bats are used. The computer compares the random number generator to the batting average. If the random number is less than or equal to the batting average, we record "Hit"; otherwise, we record "Out." Notice in Figure 12.1 that the first hit occurs in the fourth

game. Cell H11 has a random number of 0.130, which is less than 0.333. You may have noticed that cell H8 also has a value lower than 0.333; however, Game 1 only had three at-bats, so this number is not used. Continue this process for all 162 games. As an added feature, we count the number of hits in a game in column Q. In Game 4 (row 11 of the spreadsheet), the batter broke out of the slump, going 1 for 5. In Game 26 (row 33) he went 4 for 5. Column R counts the number of consecutive games with a hit. Using an "IF" statement, we add up the number of games with hits. If the value in column Q is a number other than 0, we add one to the previous value in column R. So, returning to game 4, the value in cell Q11 is a 1. The value in R10 is a 0, so we add 1 to it, creating a 1 in R11. The batter also got a hit in game 5, so the value in cell R12 is 1 + 1 = 2. Notice that from game 20 through game 40, our batter with a 0.333 batting average had a 21-game hitting streak. The maximum streak for a 162-game season can also be displayed at the top of the spreadsheet (cell K2). Finally, we can add up all of the at-bats in the simulation (in this simulation we had 642 at-bats). In addition we can add up the total number of hits (228) and determine that the batter had a seasonal batting average of .355 (shown in cell G4).

Based on observed data, we input the batting average. We can then run a simulation and determine a hitting streak and simulated batting average. With technology today, thousands of seasonal simulations can be run in minutes. Suppose we input Joe DiMaggio's batting average. During his famous streak, Joe had a batting average of .408 and a slugging average of .717. If we input this batting average into our simulation, it is likely that we still would not see a hitting streak anywhere close to 56 games.

How good of a model is our simulation? First, it does not update the batting average after each game, although this could be incorporated with some effort. Varying the batting average from game to game would give insight into whether or not the batter gets into a slump. Our simulation uses actual data from DiMaggio's 1941 season (specifically, the number of at-bats per game). This appears to be reasonable for a general approximation. The biggest point that one might bring up concerns the pitcher. During the 1941 streak, DiMaggio faced four future Hall of Fame pitchers, and yet he was successful. It is difficult to predict whether a given pitcher will be "in the zone" during a particular game. Some great batters claim they never have success against certain pitchers. However, conducting a simulation offers some insight into situations where a sabermetrical analysis might not.

Regression

As a second example of analyzing the game of baseball beyond saber-metrics, let's consider salary data. Baseball agents, general managers, and arbitrators use statistics in determining how lucrative a contract to a player should receive. Oftentimes they employ regression in determining a baseline salary. We will develop a regression model to predict future earnings based on past performances. As a basic example, consider two variables, x, and y, that represent two quantities, say batting average and salary, respectively. If the salary is based solely on batting average, we could use a linear relationship, such as $y = \beta_0 + \beta_1 x$. The slope β_1 and y-intercept β_0 determine a straight line. In this example, the batting average (x) is the independent variable, and the salary (y), is the dependent variable. Given a set of values for x, we could predict values for y in a linear fashion. In the context of our example, if we know the player's batting average, we multiply it by a constant β_1, add another constant β_0, and determine the salary. This is known as a simple linear regression model.

Player	Team	2006 Average	2006 Salary
Orlando Hudson	Arizona	0.287	$2,300,000
Marcus Giles	Atlanta	0.262	$3,850,000
Todd Walker	Chicago	0.278	$2,500,000
Jamey Carroll	Colorado	0.300	$700,000
Dan Uggla	Florida	0.282	$327,000
Craig Biggio	Houston	0.246	$4,000,000
Jeff Kent	Los Angeles	0.292	$9,400,000
Rickie Weeks	Milwaukee	0.279	$1,220,000
Jose Valentin	New York	0.271	$912,500
Chase Utley	Philadelphia	0.309	$500,000
Jose Castillo	Pittsburgh	0.253	$975,000
Josh Barfield	San Diego	0.280	$327,000
Ray Durham	San Francisco	0.293	$7,000,000
Aaron Miles	St. Louis	0.263	$350,000
Jose Vidro	Washington	0.289	$7,000,000

Table 12.3 Batting average and salary data for
2006 National League second basemen

Often players are compared to other players of equal ability to determine salary. Consider the 2006 National League second basemen. In Table 12.3, we list fifteen of the sixteen second basemen who played the most games for their respective teams in 2006, followed by their batting averages, and their 2006 salaries. Brandon Phillips was the regular second baseman for the Cincinnati Reds, batting .276. Based solely on the batting averages of his peers, what should Phillips' salary be?

The first step in developing a regression analysis that involves just two variables is to try to develop a trend for the data. We therefore create a scatter plot of the observed data (see Figure 12.2), with the independent variable, batting average, on the x-axis, and the dependent variable, salary, on the y-axis.

An initial look at the chart seems to reveal no pattern. Is there a trend? Using the method of least squares, we develop a trend line (the best fit of the data to a line). The principle behind the least squares method tells us that the vertical deviation of a point from a line is equal to the y-value of the point minus the y-value of the line for a given x-value. In other words, it is equal to $y - (\beta_0 + \beta_1 x)$. This difference is calculated for all (x, y) pairs of the data, and then each vertical deviation is squared and summed. The scatter plot is shown again in Figure 13.3, with the trend line. The equation for this line is given by $y = 24{,}481{,}096x - 4{,}071{,}161$. The point estimates of β_1 and β_0 are called the least squares estimates and are those values which minimize the sum of the squared difference between y and $(\beta_0 + \beta_1 x)$.

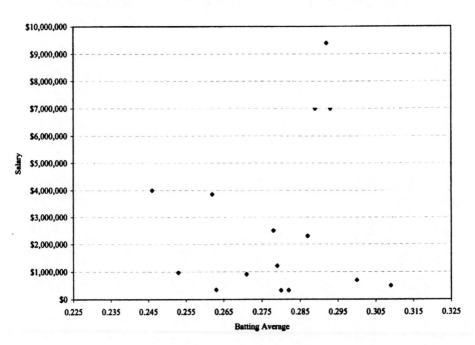

Figure 12.2 Scatterplot of batting average / salary data

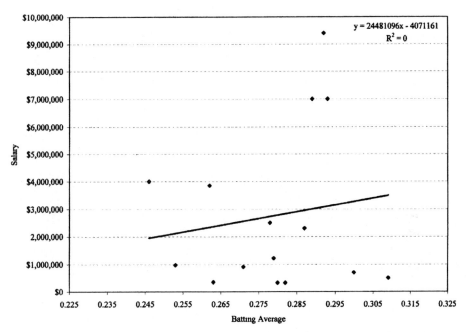

Figure 12.3 Scatterplot with trend line

How good is this trend line? In truth, for this model it's not very good at all. The equation basically states that a ballplayer would have to owe over four million dollars if he never had an at-bat, or if his batting average remained at .000. Substituting Brandon Phillips' batting average of .276, he should have made $2,685,621. However, both Rickie Weeks and Todd Walker had batting averages close to but greater than Phillips', but their 2006 salaries were less than the prediction for Phillips. Further, only five players have salaries above the predicted line.

What happened? First, trying to predict something as complicated as a salary based on only one independent variable is probably not going to work. Second, the fifteen data points were spread out, with a maximum value of $9,400,000 and a minimum value of $327,000 (the league minimum). The mean for the data is $2,757,433, but the standard deviation is $2,915,708, which is larger than the mean! The player with the highest batting average had one of the lowest salaries, and several high-paid players had lower batting averages. Additionally, there were only 15 sets of data points. To get a more accurate prediction we need more data.

Let's not give up yet. We wish to find a parameter that has a lower variability in the regression model. If the variability is small, the data points will tend to be closer to the predicted regression line, and the sum of the squared error (vertical deviation) will be small. Most statistics texts give thorough explanations of the sum of squared error, often denoted by "SSE," and the reader should consult a statistics text for greater details. Our purpose here is to say that a useful estimate of the variance of the data can be calculated from the SSE:

$$\hat{\sigma}^2 = \frac{SSE}{n-2},$$

where $\hat{\sigma}^2$ is the estimate of the variance, SSE is the sum of squared error, and n is the number of data points. The denominator in the above expression gives the number of degrees of freedom associated with the variance estimate. The SSE can often be thought of as how the variation in the dependent variable y is unexplained in the linear relationship. Or, how much the data cannot be modeled by a linear relationship. If the SSE or variance estimate $\hat{\sigma}^2$ is relatively high, as in the above example, the data probably cannot be modeled with a linear regression model. We can quantitatively measure the total amount of variation in the observed y-values by calculating the "SST," the total sum of squares, where SST equals the sum of the y-values squared minus the sum of the y-values squared divided by n:

$$SST = \sum y^2 - \frac{\left(\sum y^2\right)}{n}$$

for each y-value. After calculating the SSE and SST, we can determine the coefficient of determination, or r^2 value, as follows:

$$r^2 = 1 - \frac{SSE}{SST}.$$

The closer to 1 the value of r^2, the better the fit of the data to a simple linear regression model. Further, most current statistical programs provide the r^2 value as part of the descriptive statistics output.

Rather than try to find one variable which can accurately predict another, let's attempt to build a model which takes as its input several independent variables (x_i) and then predicts one dependent variable y. We will add up the independent variables (multiplied by different coefficients) and then create a model. For example, perhaps runs batted in can be predicted by using home runs, triples, and doubles. We assign a variable to each independent variable and our general additive multiple regression model becomes

$$y = \beta_0 + \beta_1 x_1 + \beta_2 x_2 + \beta_3 x_3 + \varepsilon,$$

where x_1 corresponds to the number of home runs in a season, x_2 corresponds to triples, and x_3 are doubles. One might believe that a high number of extra-base hits correlates to a high number of RBIs. Let's see if it's true. There is still some error (ε) associated with this method. All of the independent variables appear linearly in this expression. This is the simplest multiple regression model. The dependent variable y is a linear function and we get a deviation from the expression by some amount known as the error. Notice that there is no interaction among the independent variables. Other multiple regression models exist which offer no interaction or complete interaction among the variables. For example,

$$y = \beta_0 + \beta_1 x_1 + \beta_2 x_2 + \beta_3 x_1^2 + \beta_4 x_2^2 + \varepsilon$$

is a model which is now nonlinear but has no interaction between x_1 and x_2. On the other hand,

$$y = \beta_0 + \beta_1 x_1 + \beta_2 x_2 + \beta_3 x_1 x_2 + \varepsilon$$

shows interaction between x_1 and x_2 and is thus nonlinear (we could also add a term which has x_1^2 or x_2^2, if desirable). Further, the powers of each variable need not be integers. Nonlinear multiple regression models can be very complicated, and we will not explore them further in this discussion.

Player	Year	H	2B	3B	HR	XBH	RBI
Babe Ruth	1921	204	44	16	59	119	171
Lou Gehrig	1927	218	52	18	47	117	175
Chuck Klein	1930	250	59	8	40	107	170
Barry Bonds	2001	156	32	2	73	107	137
Todd Helton	2001	197	54	2	49	105	146
Chuck Klein	1932	226	50	15	38	103	137
H Greenberg	1937	200	49	14	40	103	183
Stan Musial	1948	230	46	18	39	103	131
Albert Belle	1995	173	52	1	50	103	126
Todd Helton	2000	216	59	2	42	103	147
Sammy Sosa	2001	189	34	5	64	103	160
Rogers Hornsby	1922	250	46	14	42	102	152
Lou Gehrig	1930	220	42	17	41	100	174
Jimmie Foxx	1932	213	33	9	58	100	169
Luis Gonzalez	2001	198	36	7	57	100	142
Carlos Delgado	2000	196	57	1	41	99	137

Table 12.4 Top extra-base hits leaders in a single season

As an example, there have only been fifteen times when a major league player has had 100 or more extra-base hits in a season. The first to do it was Babe Ruth in 1921, and his record of 119 extra-base hits in a single season still stands. Amazingly, four occurrences sprung out of the 2001 season. Just below this extraordinary listing of players are eight occurrences of 99 extra-base hits, including twice by Babe Ruth. Carlos Delgado is also one of the "not-quite-100" extra-base-hit players. Suppose we wished to calculate how many RBIs Carlos Delgado should have had in 2004, given his extra-base hit data. Let's compare his statistics to those 15 best extra-base hit seasons. In Table 13.4 (on page 125) we list the players.

In trying to predict the number of runs batted in, we determine that the intercept, β_0, should equal 74.509, and the other three coefficients are as follows: $\beta_1 = 0.612$, $\beta_2 = 1.765$, and $\beta_3 = 0.704$. Putting this all together, the prediction for runs batted in becomes

$$\text{RBIs} = 74.509 + 0.612 \times 2\text{B} + 1.765 \times 3\text{B} + 0.704 \times \text{HR}.$$

If we substitute Babe Ruth's 1921 totals into the equation, we find that he should have had $74.509 + 0.612 \times 44 + 1.765 \times 16 + 0.704 \times 59 = 171$ RBIs, which is exactly his actual 1921 total of 171. Todd Helton's 2001 season also predicts an RBI total of 146, his actual amount. What about Carlos Delgado? Based upon this multiple regression, his predicted RBI total should have been 140, which is within three of his actual total of 137.

Notice that the RBI equation listed above predicts 74 runs batted in, even if the player has no extra-base hits (substitute a zero in for the number of doubles, triples, and home runs). Also, the higher the value of the variable for the data sets, the less impact the coefficient has. Notice that the average number of doubles is higher than the average number of home runs for our 100+ extra-base hit sluggers. The average number of triples is much lower. So, the coefficients for triples is higher than that for home runs, which is slightly higher than that for doubles.

Suppose we had tried to model RBIs based solely on the number of extra-base hits (predict the last column of Table 12.4 using the second-to-last column only). Two scatter plots of extra-base hits versus runs batted in are shown in Figure 12.4 and Figure 12.5, along with a trend line (we used a simple linear regression model). In Figure 12.4, we use only those data sets corresponding to at least 100 extra-base hits. In Figure 12.5, we include all data corresponding to 90 or more extra-base hits in a season.

This scatter plot's trend line has an r^2 value of only 0.0997, which is not valuable. By using a multiple regression model on the data in Table 12.4, the r^2 value increases to almost 24 percent (still not that good). However, when more data points are used (for example, when using the top 62 occurrences which equate to the seasons in which a batter had at least 90 extra-base hits), the r^2 value increases to about 33 percent.

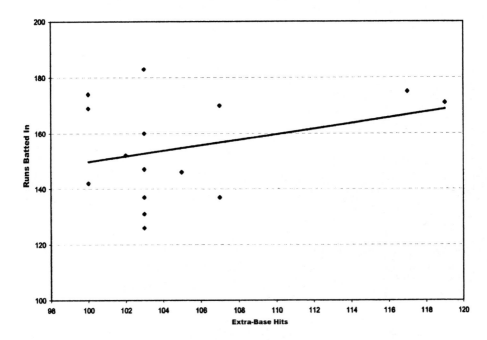

Figure 12.4 Scatterplot of extra-base hits versus runs batted in, top 15

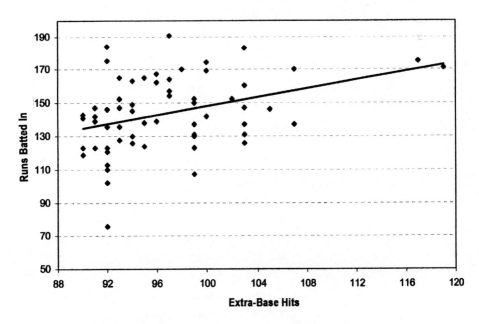

Figure 12.5 Scatterplot of extra-base hits versus runs batted in, top 62

Many fans may argue that more is involved in predicting RBIs. Perhaps that is true. Perhaps we should use a nonlinear regression model. Or, perhaps we should use other variables, such as split statistics. For example, what is a batter's chance of driving in a run when runners are in scoring position? The above regression model does not take into account any runners being on base. Therefore, the only way a run will be batted in with no one on base is if the batter hits a home run and drives himself in. With the recent availability of data on the Internet, we could gather information about how many times a batter steps up to the plate with runners on base. That information could be factored into a regression model. The more data we wish to use as independent variables, the more complicated the model will become.

There are data sets that fit regression lines in a better way. Let's consider runs scored by a team in a season. The table below shows the runs scored, with on-base percentage (OBP), slugging percentage (SLG) and the popular on-base plus slugging percentage (OPS).

Runs	OBP	SLG	OPS
930	0.363	0.461	0.824
870	0.349	0.457	0.806
868	0.342	0.464	0.806
865	0.347	0.447	0.794
849	0.337	0.455	0.791
835	0.338	0.446	0.784
834	0.334	0.445	0.780
822	0.329	0.449	0.777
820	0.351	0.435	0.786
820	0.348	0.432	0.781
813	0.341	0.433	0.774
809	0.348	0.463	0.811
801	0.347	0.425	0.771
781	0.337	0.431	0.769
773	0.331	0.424	0.755
771	0.340	0.412	0.752
768	0.339	0.424	0.763
766	0.334	0.425	0.759
758	0.331	0.435	0.766
757	0.332	0.411	0.743
756	0.325	0.424	0.749
749	0.336	0.432	0.768

Runs	OBP	SLG	OPS
746	0.338	0.418	0.756
746	0.324	0.422	0.746
735	0.332	0.409	0.741
731	0.332	0.416	0.749
730	0.327	0.420	0.747
716	0.319	0.422	0.741
691	0.327	0.397	0.723
689	0.314	0.420	0.733

Table 12.5 Offensive data, 2006

Let's try to fit both a single-variable linear regression and a multi-variable linear regression equation to this set of data. First, we show a scatter plot of the data (OPS versus runs scored) in Figure 12.6. The data appears to exhibit a trend: as the OPS of a team increases, the number of runs scored also increases.

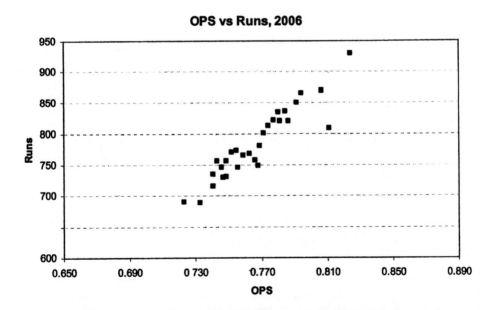

Figure 12.6. Scatterplot of OPS versus runs for the 2006 season

Fitting a trend line to the data gives encouraging results. In Figure 12.8, we again show the data with the trend line based on the least squares method. The equation of the line is

$$\text{Runs} = 2159.7 \times \text{OPS} - 872.41$$

The coefficient of correlation is over 87 percent. This is a valid example of applying a linear regression to data using a single independent variable (OPS).

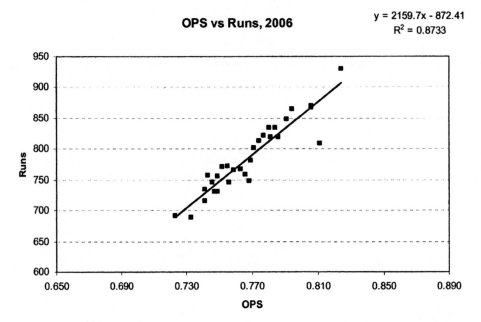

Figure 12.7 Scatterplot of OPS versus runs with trend line for the 2006 season

As mentioned earlier, we would like to apply this technique to more data. In Figure 13.8, we show a scatter plot of OPS versus runs scored for five seasons, 2002 through 2006. The data appears to exhibit a strong trend. The equation of the regression line is now

$$\text{Runs} = 2171.3 \times \text{OPS} - 877.37$$

This equation is very similar to the one developed for just the 2006 data. In addition, the R^2 value has increased to 89.66 percent, or almost 90 percent.

Next we try to model the runs-scored data with multiple variables. We will use a simple linear model, where we attempt to predict runs as a function of both on-base average (OBA) and slugging percentage (SLG), given by

$$\text{Runs} = \beta_0 + \beta_1 \times \text{OBA} + \beta_2 \times \text{SLG}$$

Using just the 2006 data (30 data points), we find that the regression equation is given by Runs = − 924.30 + 2585.19 × OBA + 1948.31 × SLG,

OPS vs Runs, 2002 to 2006

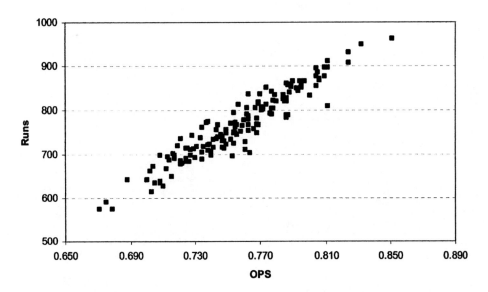

Figure 12.8 Scatterplot of OPS versus runs for the 2002 to 2006 seasons

which yields a correlation coefficient of 87.78 percent, or almost half a percent better than using single-variable regression. Using all 150 data points from the 2002 through 2006 seasons, we develop a regression equation of Runs = − 948.02 + 2696.44 × OBA + 1925.21 × SLG, which yields a correlation coefficient of 90.00 percent, again slightly better than using single-variable regression. The coefficients for each independent variable do not change significantly when more data is added.

We hope that we have provided an introduction into simulation and regression which will allow the reader to get started in analyzing baseball data. It is not a trivial process, but it can offer insights which might not be available using commonly-accepted sabermetrical measures.

Easy Tosses

1. Create a simulation in which a batter has an equal chance of getting 2, 3, 4, or 5 at-bats in a game (assume that he will get only one of those outcomes). Use a batting average of .300 and simulate a 150-game season (our batter sits out a few games during the season). After the simulation, how does the simulated batting average compare to the input batting average?

2. Several studies have been done to predict runs scored using offensive measures such as RBIs, OPS, and batting average. Select thirty players with a similar number of at-bats from a given season and try to predict the runs scored.

Clubhouse:
Answers to Problems

Infield Practice: Sabermetrical Reasoning

Fast Ball Down the Middle

Before the 1990s, Pirate Hall of Famer Ralph Kiner had the second-best career home run percentage behind Babe Ruth (with Harmon Kille-brew a tad behind Kiner). Ruth was the first player in history to hit 30, 40, 50 and 60 home runs in a season. Following 1961, and some years after, many people still argued that Ruth, not Roger Maris, held the seasonal home record, due to the extended 1961 season (162 games versus 154 games in Ruth's time). Ruth held the season home run percentage mark as well.

Over the past ten years or so, however, sluggers like Sammy Sosa, Mark McGwire and Barry Bonds have surpassed many of Ruth's accomplishments. Apart from the questions and controversies which have been raised, one fact seems to endure. No player in history has out-homered teams 90 times; or pairs of teams, which Ruth accomplished 18 times. It would seem that Ruth is still mighty and still prevails.

Inning 1: Simple Additive Formulas

Easy Tosses

(1)

	Bonds
BA	0.299
OBP	0.443
SLG	0.608
POP	1.35

(2)

	Pujols	*Howard*	*Morneau*
BA	0.331	0.313	0.321
OB	0.431	0.425	0.375
SLG	0.671	0.659	0.559
POP	1.433	1.397	1.255

(3)

	HEQ-O
Molina	226
Pujols	668
Miles	247
Rolen	494
Eckstein	285.5
Edmonds	317.5

Sample calculation: Pujols: HEQ-O = TB + R + RBI + SB + 0.5 × BB = 359 + 119 + 137 + 7 + 0.5 × 92 = 668

(4)

	POS	*PMF*	*HEQD*
Molina	C	0.445	432.10
Pujols	1B	0.51	407.62
Miles	2B	0.46	200.1
Rolen	3B	0.888	366.74
Eckstein	SS	0.548	337.57
Edmonds	OF	none	233

Sample calculation: Molina: HEQ-D = C: (PO + 3 A + 2 DP − 2 E) × (0.445) = (736 + 3(77) + 2(6) − 2(4)) × (0.445) = 432.095.

If Molina's putouts were greater than 800, we would have assigned him 800 putouts.

(5)

	HEQ-O	*HEQ-D*	*PMT*
Molina	226	432.10	658.10
Pujols	668	407.62	1075.62
Miles	247	200.1	447.1
Rolen	494	366.74	860.74
Eckstein	285.5	337.57	623.07
Edmonds	317.5	233	550.5

(6) Total Average = (TB + BB + HBP + SB) / (AB – H + SH + SF + CS + GIDP)

Pujols: (359 + 92 + 4 + 7) / (535 – 177 + 0 + 3 + 2 + 20) = 1.2063

Howard: (383 + 108 + 9 + 0) / (581 – 182 + 0 + 6 + 0 + 7) = 1.2136

Hard Sliders

(1)

1	*AL66*	*FROB*	*NL54*	*WMAYS*
BA	0.24	0.316	0.265	0.345
OBP	0.306	0.41	0.335	0.411
SLG	0.369	0.637	0.407	0.667
POP	0.915	1.363	1.007	1.423

Thus, in 1966, the AL had a POP of .915 and Robinson's was 1.363. Thus, his relative POP was 1.363 / 0.915 = 1.490 , meaning that Robinson's POP was 49 percent better than the league average.

In 1954, the NL POP was 1.007, Mays's 1.423, so his relative POP was 1.423 / 1.007 = 1.413, meaning that Mays's POP was 41 percent better than the league average.

(2)

	NL01	*Bonds*	*AL21*	*Ruth*
TA	0.725	1.89	0.693	1.77
Rel TA		2.61		2.55

These players' total averages are more than 250 percent better than their leagues' figures. Bonds was about 261 percent better than the league in 2001, and Ruth was about 255 percent better than the league in 1921.

(3) One suggestion: (POP × 1000) + (TA × 1000) + PMT, to put things roughly on a scale in which 3000 is excellent.

Inning 2: Peak vs. Career Performances

An Inside Pitch

This is a tough one. Few people would doubt that Barry Bonds is the best player of these three sluggers. And of late he has had arguably the greatest offensive seasons ever. However, he broke the 50 home run mark only once (when he hit 73 in 2001). Mark McGwire, on the other hand, has the best career home run frequency of all time, and he four times hit 50 home runs in a season (hitting 60 or more twice). Yet, a strong case can be made for Sammy Sosa, with respect to home run peak value. He is the only player in history to hit 60+ home runs three times, not to mention a 50 home run season in 2000.

An Outside Pitch

With all respect to Heilmann (4 batting titles in the 1920s), the seven crowns won by Musial and the eight titles garnered by Gwynn, it is difficult to rank Cobb anywhere but first with respect to batting titles. He won a dozen titles in 13 years, facing competition from such hitters as Tris Speaker, Nap Lajoie and Joe Jackson (who sported lifetime batting averages of .345, .338, and .356, respectively). Cobb's lifetime average is nearly 8 points better than runner-up Rogers Hornsby. And he batted less than .300 only once in 24 seasons.

A Fork Ball

John, Blyleven, Kaat, and Morris had career victory totals of 288, 287, 283, and 254, respectively. In 26 years, Tommy John was a 4-time All-Star and twice came in second in Cy Young Award voting. He won 20 or more games in a season only three times, and his winning percentage was .555. In 22 seasons, Bert Blyleven was a 2-time All-Star, and twice came in third place in Cy Young Award voting. He won 20 games in a season only once and finished with a .534 winning percentage. In 25 seasons, Jim Kaat was voted to only one All-Star game and received votes only once for the Cy Young Award. He won 20 or more games in a season three times, and his winning percentage was .544. Jack Morris pitched 18 years in the major leagues, garnering five All-Star appearances, receiving votes for the Cy Young Award seven times (highest place was third, and it happened twice) and league MVP Award six times. He won 20 or more games in a season three times, and his winning percentage was .577. Despite his shortage of wins compared to the other three, Jack Morris could be argued as having the best career value. In addition, he has three World Series rings, as many as the other three hurlers combined.

An Intentional Walk

Here is the data on the Pittsburgh Pirates:

Year	RS	RA	ERA	BA	OBP	SLG
1990	733	619	3.40	.259	.331	.405
1991	768	632	3.44	.263	.338	.398
1992	693	595	3.35	.255	.324	.381

Barry Bonds won the MVP Award in 1990 and 1992, placing 2nd in 1991. The OPS for 1990 and 1991 are identical, with little difference in ERA and runs. Both 1990 and 1991 teams had only one 20-game winner. The 1990 Cincinnati Reds beat the Pirates and went on to win the World Series, while the Braves beat the Pirates the next two years, only to lose in the Series to Minnesota and Toronto. Bonds went 13 for 68 in the three series, posting a sub-.200 batting average, while the Pirates themselves, batted .194, .224, and .255 in the three series.

Hit and Run

Here is the data:

Team	W	L	RS	RA	Finish
1998 Yankees	108	54	965	656	1st in AL East, won WS
2001 Mariners	116	46	927	627	1st in NL West, lost ALCS
2003 Braves	101	61	907	740	1st in NL East, lost Div Series

The Yankees obviously won it all, which is the goal of every team. The Mariners proved to be a disappointment, losing the ALCS to the New York Yankees in five games.

Inning 3: The Equivalence Coefficient

Easy Tosses

(1) We find that Greenberg would get 4257 additional at bats. The kicker of 1.02 gives an equivalence coefficient of 1.836. Multiplying this by 331 gives a projected home run total of 608.

(2) Don Mattingly would get an additional 4067 at bats; the kicker of 1.01 yields an equivalence coefficient of 1.589. Mattingly had 2153 hits in his career; his projected total would be 3416.

(3) Koufax's earned run average goes down from 2.76 to 2.72. In the 1200 additional innings, he would have given up 368 earned runs; the kicker is 1.04.

(4) J.R.'s new ERA becomes 3.09; The kicker is 1.05. His additional strike-outs are 976, giving him a new strikeout total of 1493 + 976 = 2469.

Hard Slider

(1) The Splendid Splinter's projected totals are: 3377 hits, 665 home runs and a batting average of .349.

(2) Warren Spahn's kicker is 0.95. By giving him 750 additional IP, he would have won 52 additional games. Multiplying 52 by 0.95, we see that Spahn would have won 49 games in the three seasons he missed, giving him a total of 363 + 49 = 412, or just 5 wins behind Walter Johnson.

Inning 4: The Linear Weights School — Offense

Easy Tosses

(1)

Player	Season	Lindsey SLG
Ty Cobb	1911	0.955
Lou Gehrig	1931	0.917
Babe Ruth	1921	0.907
Ted Williams	1941	0.929

(2)

Player	1983	LW
Cal Ripken		43.28
Eddie Murray		54.05

(3)

Player	1960	LW
Smoky Burgess		9.79
Dick Stuart		14.51
Bill Mazeroski		4.88
Don Hoak		25.2
Dick Groat		14.76
Roberto Clemente		22.2
Bob Skinner		14.99
Bill Virdon		6.83

Answers to Problems 139

(4)

Year	AL MVP	OPS	League Leader in OPS	WS OPS Leader
1995	Mo Vaughn	0.963	Edgar Martinez — 1.107	Fred McGriff — 0.850
1996	Juan Gonzalez	1.011	Mark McGwire — 1.198	Bernie Williams — 0.926
1997	Ken Griffey, Jr.	1.028	Frank Thomas — 1.067	Gary Sheffield — 0.870
1998	Juan Gonzalez	0.996	Albert Belle — 1.055	Bernie Williams — 0.997
1999	Ivan Rodriguez	0.914	Manny Ramirez — 1.105	Derek Jeter — 0.990
2000	Jason Giambi	1.113	Manny Ramirez — 1.154	Bernie Williams — 0.957
2001	Ichiro Suzuki	0.838	Jason Giambi — 1.137	Luis Gonzalez — 1.117
2002	Miguel Tejada	0.862	Jim Thome — 1.122	Tim Salmon — 0.883

Hard Slider

(1)

Player	Year	LW
Aaron	1957	60.63
Bonds	1990	56.72
Ruth	1923	134.66
Mays	1954	81.31
Sosa	1998	73.81

(2)

	AB	H	2B	3B	HR	1B	BB	HBP	LWBR
Roger Bresnahan	4481	1252	218	71	26	937	714	67	174.70
Buck Ewing	5363	1625	250	178	72	1125	392	9	216.40
Ray Shalk	5306	1345	199	49	11	1086	638	59	−25.79

(3)

	AB	H	2B	3B	HR	1B	BB	HBP	LWBR
Earl Webb	589	196	67	3	14	112	70	0	52.62
George Burns	603	216	64	3	4	145	28	8	42.07
Joe Medwick	636	223	64	13	18	128	34	4	58.74
Hank Greenberg	593	201	63	7	26	105	87	2	73.89
Paul Waner	630	215	62	10	8	135	56	2	49.30
Charlie Gehringer	641	227	60	12	15	140	83	4	71.89

It looks like Hank Greenberg contributed 7.389 wins to the Tigers in 1934.

Inning 5: The Linear Weights School —
Pitching and Defense

Easy Tosses

(1)

	PR
Mike Cuellar	9.09
Pat Dobson	14.43
Jim Palmer	21.31
Dave McNally	11.71

(2)

	PR
Alexander	47.11
Bradley	58.57
Coombs	41.97
Gibson	60.26

(4)

	G	PO	A	E	DP	Inn	FR
Bob Gibson	528	291	484	42	46	3884.3	126.3
Greg Maddux	687	516	1099	50	90	4676.3	275.4

This translates to about 0.29 runs saved per nine innings for Gibson and 0.53 runs saved per nine innings for Maddux.

Hard Slider

(2)

	ERA	W	L	CG	SHO	IP	H	R	ER	LgERA	PR
Valenzuela 1981	2.48	13	7	11	8.0	192.3	140	55	53	3.32	17.95
Valenzuela 1982	2.87	19	13	18	4	285.0	247	105	91	3.46	18.68
Gooden 1984	2.60	17	9	7	3	218.0	161	72	63	3.56	23.25
Gooden 1985	1.53	17	6	12	2	250.0	197	92	79	3.45	53.33
Nomo 1995	2.54	13	6	4	3	191.3	124	63	54	3.81	26.99
Nomo 1996	3.19	16	11	3	2	228.3	180	93	81	3.84	16.49
Willis 2003	3.30	14	6	2	2	160.7	148	61	59	4.03	13.03
Willis 2004	4.02	10	11	2	0	197.0	219	99	88	4.10	1.75

Doc Gooden's 1985 performance ranks very high on the all-time list. Dontrelle Willis could be classified as having experienced the sophomore jinx.

However, he returned to the top the next season (2005), going 22–10, with an ERA over 1.4 runs below the league average.

Inning 6: The Runs-Created School

Easy Tosses

(1a)

	W	L	PCT	G	R	OR	old expo	pythag1	plproj	w(rdd)	l
98 TEX	88	74	0.543	162	940	871	2	0.538	87.16	87	75
98 TOR	88	74	0.543	162	816	768	2	0.530	85.90	86	76

Texas's projected wins based on the Pythagorean record was 87, while Toronto's was 86.

(1b)

	W	L	PCT	G	R	OR	old expo	pythag1	plproj	w(rdd)	l	w-proj W
98 nyy	114	48	0.704	162	965	656	2	0.684	110.80	111	51	3
98 bos	92	70	0.568	162	876	729	2	0.591	95.71	96	66	−4
98 sea	76	85	0.472	161	859	855	2	0.502	80.88	81	80	−5
98 chw	80	82	0.494	162	861	931	2	0.461	74.68	75	87	5
98 cle	89	73	0.549	162	850	779	2	0.544	88.05	88	74	1
98 bal	79	83	0.488	162	817	785	2	0.520	84.23	84	78	−5
98 oak	74	88	0.457	162	804	866	2	0.463	74.99	75	87	−1
98 ana	85	77	0.525	162	787	783	2	0.503	81.41	81	81	4
98 min	70	92	0.432	162	734	818	2	0.446	72.26	72	90	−2
98 det	65	97	0.401	162	722	863	2	0.412	66.70	67	95	−2
98 kcr	72	89	0.447	161	714	899	2	0.387	62.27	62	99	10
98 tb	63	99	0.389	162	620	751	2	0.405	65.66	66	96	−3

The Kansas City Royals won 10 games more than their projection, and the Seattle Mariners and Baltimore Orioles each won 5 games fewer than their projections.

(2) We use basic runs created: $(H + BB) \times (TB) / (AB + BB) = (21276 + 7737) \times (33837) / (78416 + 7737) = 11395$ (rounded). The league scored 11365, so the runs-created figure is well within half of 1 percent of the actual figure.

(3) Bobby Murcer in 1971:

	TB	BRC	SBRC	TECHRC
Murcer	287	123.1	123.5	126.4

(4)

	HDG23	adjHDG23
Murray	126.62	121.2
Ripken	119.36	116.9

Murray seems to have created more runs, even with the adjustment

$$\frac{(A+2.4C)(B+3C)}{9C} - 0.9C$$

(5)

	W	L	RS	RA	Pythagorean Wins x = 1.82	Pythagorean Wins x = 2
April	20	5	138	89	17	18
May	20	7	172	126	17	18
June	18	9	170	131	17	17
July	18	9	135	87	19	19
August	20	9	153	103	20	20
September	15	6	115	76	14	15
October	5	1	44	15	5	5
				Wins	109	111

Hard Sliders

(1)

Player	Year	RC Formula	(a) RC	(b) Outs	(c) "Games"	(c) RC/27
Aaron	1957	HDG23	198	433	16.04	8.50
Bonds	1990	HDG23	156	377	13.96	9.34
Ruth	1923	HDG12	205	320	12.54	18.12
Mays	1954	HDG22	195	389	14.41	10.47
Sosa	1998	HDG23	198	470	17.41	8.55

Ruth had almost twice as many runs created per game as the other sluggers.

(2)

	TB	HDG23	Outs	Games	OWP	Wins
Murcer	287	127.2534	367	13.59259	0.84566	136.9969

Murcer had an offensive winning percentage of .846, or 137 wins in a 162-game season.

(3) Here is the data for Mark McGwire's rookie season (1987):

AB	H	SB	CS	BB	K	BA	TB	SH	SF	IBB	HBP	GDP
557	161	1	1	71	131	0.29	344	0	8	8	5	6

From these numbers, his RC = 127.1 runs, his RCTECH = 131.5 runs, and his HDG23 = 130.8 runs. All are pretty close.

Inning 7: Win Shares

Easy Tosses

(1a)

AL98	MR-O	MR-D	TOT
NYY	559.105	561.685	1120.79
TEX	534.105	346.685	880.79
BOS	470.105	488.685	958.79
SEA	453.105	362.685	815.79
CHW	455.105	286.685	741.79
CLE	444.105	438.685	882.79
BAL	411.105	432.685	843.79
TOR	410.105	449.685	859.79
OAK	398.105	351.685	749.79
ANA	381.105	434.685	815.79
MIN	328.105	399.685	727.79
DET	316.105	354.685	670.79
KC	308.105	318.685	626.79
TB	214.105	466.685	680.79

(1b)

AL98	pythag#	pythprojW	MR Proj	MR projW
NYY	0.684	110.8	0.690	111.8
TEX	0.591	95.7	0.543	87.9
BOS	0.544	88.1	0.591	95.7
SEA	0.538	87.2	0.502	80.9
CHW	0.530	85.9	0.457	74.5
CLE	0.503	81.4	0.544	88.1
BAL	0.461	74.7	0.520	84.2
TOR	0.520	84.2	0.530	86.3
OAK	0.502	80.9	0.462	74.8
ANA	0.463	75.0	0.502	81.4
MIN	0.387	62.3	0.448	72.6
DET	0.446	72.3	0.413	66.9
KC	0.412	66.7	0.386	62.2
TB	0.405	65.7	0.419	67.9

Hard Sliders and Split-Fingered Fastball

Win Shares Long-Form Answers:

Name	Win Shares	Name	Win Shares
Hernandez	29	Johnson	10
Strawberry	25	Heep	8
Carter	23	Santana	8
Dykstra	23	Teufel	8
Ojeda	18	Aguilera	6
Darling	17	Foster	6
Gooden	17	Anderson	4
Knight	17	Hearn	4
Backman	16	Sisk	4
McDowell	16	Gibbons	3
Wilson	16	Mazzilli	3
Mitchell	14	Niemann	2
Orosco	13	Elster	1
Fernandez	12	Magadan	1

Seventh-Inning Stretch: Non-Sabermetrical Factors

A Hot-Stove League Question

In no particular order:

- Should individual records be expunged if it proved that steroids and/or other "enhancing" factors have been used by players?
- Should aluminum bats be used?
- Should managers have the option to appeal to video replay with respect to controversial rulings by umpires?
- Will countries in Asia, Latin America, etc. have major league franchises?
- Should there be a salary cap in major league baseball?
- Why not count all records, even if games are stopped before five innings, by just picking up the game where it was suspended? (Under Rule 4.10 of the official rules of Major League Baseball, a game is declared "No Game" if the umpire calls it before five innings have been completed or if the home team trails the visiting team and has not completed its fifth at-bat. All statistics are discounted.)
- When one considers interleague play, wild cards, teams changing leagues (i.e., the Milwaukee Brewers), and other factors, has baseball become "footballized"?
- Is baseball still the national pastime?

A Fantasy League Question

Whatever you as president of the National League decide, don't use an asterisk!

Inning 8: Park Effects

Easy Tosses

(1)

> Crawford, 52.28; adj, 53.85
> Jones, 101.13; adj, 103.15
> Williams, 126.99; adj, 120.00

(2a)

> Betamit: 21.66
> Wright: 119.15
> ARamirez: 115.22

(2b)

Betamit: 21.12
Wright: 125.11
ARamirez: 111.18

(3a)

BOS: 1.13
OAK: 0.83

(3b)

Yastrzemski: 113.31
Reynolds: 34.51

(3c)

Yastrzemski: 105.95
Reynolds: 37.44

(4a)

Team	H-RS	H-RA	R-RS	R-RA	PF	
CIN	407	373	386	390	1.01	H
PIT	324	322	401	330	0.88	P
ChC	382	317	333	290	1.12	H
SF	362	317	351	319	1.01	H
ATL	360	321	331	310	1.06	H
HOU	371	313	305	355	1.04	H
LaD	325	258	320	303	0.94	P
Phi	317	378	328	367	1	N
NYM	308	266	324	275	0.96	P
StL	276	276	318	264	0.95	P
MON	288	421	294	370	1.07	H
SD	239	358	229	388	0.97	P

(4b) Repeat the directions for part (a) for the NL in 2006.

Team	H-RS	H-RA	R-RS	R-RA	PF	
PHI	444	420	421	392	1.06	H
ATL	414	390	435	415	0.95	P
NYM	395	347	439	384	0.9	P
LaD	438	365	382	386	1.05	H
COL	456	413	357	399	1.15	H
StL	404	352	382	414	0.95	P

Team	H-RS	H-RA	R-RS	R-RA	PF	
ARI	403	429	370	359	1.14	H
FLA	353	371	405	401	0.9	P
SF	382	388	369	407	0.99	P
CIN	401	429	348	372	1.15	H
WAS	373	412	373	460	0.94	P
HOU	372	367	363	352	1.03	H
MIL	385	398	345	435	1	N
SD	315	337	416	342	0.86	P
ChC	374	429	342	405	1.07	H
PIT	380	367	311	430	1.01	H

Hard Slider

(a) Calculate the PF for Fenway Park for each season from 1996–2006.

Year	H-RS	H-RA	R-RS	R-RA	PF
1996	517	464	411	457	1.13
1997	428	421	423	436	0.988
1998	439	364	437	365	1.001
1999	453	361	383	357	1.1
2000	394	380	398	365	1.014
2001	391	378	381	367	1.015
2002	396	353	463	312	0.966
2003	532	395	429	414	1.1

Anomaly: Fenway was a pitchers' park in 1997 and 2002.

Inning 9: Creating Measures and Doing Sabermetrics — Some Examples

Powerful Quests

(1) In volume 34 of the *Baseball Research Journal* (SABR, 2005), we three authors published an article titled "Cumulative Home Run Frequency and the Recent Home Run Explosion." In it, we considered all 500+ career home run hitters. In all but four cases, these sluggers seemed to have their cumulative home run ratio level off by the time they were 30 years of age. The

only exceptions were: Barry Bonds, Mark McGwire, Rafael Palmeiro and Sammy Sosa.

(2) Riordan's instrument is very revealing. It gives a method to compare players from eras, thus providing a way to measure such things as "dominance" and "relativity." It can be used either with cumulative statistics, such as hits, stolen bases, wins, saves, and errors, or with percentage statistics such as fielding average, batting average and earned run average. The calculations of peer-ratios would be very time-consuming without the Internet.

(3) Many factors come into play when studying the statistic K/9IP. There appears to be no correlation between having a large number of strikeouts and winning percentage. Also, the number of innings pitched for the single-season leaders are nowhere close to being uniform. However, in recent years, the league leaders are posting impressive strikeout numbers with an equally impressive number of innings. This discussion can go in many directions.

Easy Tosses

(1) Hank Greenberg has the highest ISO.

	BA	*SLG*	*ISO*
Earl Webb	0.333	0.528	0.195
George Burns	0.358	0.494	0.136
Joe Medwick	0.351	0.577	0.226
Hank Greenberg	0.339	0.600	0.261
Paul Waner	0.341	0.510	0.168
Charlie Gehringer	0.354	0.555	0.201

(2)

Gibson: 3.58 / 2.18 = 1.63
Clemens: 4.14 / 1.87 = 2.21

Clemens had a better season, based solely on ERA relative to the league, than Gibson, which is hard to believe.

(3)

Blair in 1969: 2.81 RF, compared to a Lg RF of 1.84
Jones in 1969: 1.86 RF, compared to a Lg RF of 1.75

Blair, career in OF: 2.37 RF, compared to a Lg RF of 1.95
Jones, career in OF: 1.86 RF, compared to a Lg RF of 1.85

The Mets should have kept Blair.

Appendix: Sabermetrics in the Classroom — A Primer

What follows is an educational primer, the purpose of which is to assist in the teaching and learning of sabermetrics in a more formal context — that is, in the classroom. We share with you our techniques and approaches and give our pedagogical views. We invite you to adapt anything contained in this primer to your specific educational situation. This would apply to both lecture-hall classes and one-on-one individual studies.

Please feel free to contact us at the following e-mail addresses:

- Gabriel B. Costa: gabriel.costa@usma.edu
- Michael R. Huber: huber@muhlenberg.edu
- John T. Saccoman: saccomjt@shu.edu

We would be happy to provide guidance and respond to questions or concerns.

This primer is divided into the following sections:

(A) Review and Overview of Sabermetrics Courses

(B) Prerequisites for Courses on Sabermetrics

(C) Course Objectives

(D) Course Content

(E) In-class Dynamics

(F) Data Mining and Course Aids

(G) Outside Speakers and Panels

(H) Field Trips

(I) Sample of Assessment Instruments: Some Supplemental Problems, Projects, and Examinations

(J) Student Feedback

(A) Review and Overview of Sabermetrics Courses

As we mentioned in our acknowledgments, we believe that the first course on sabermetrics was offered in the 1988 Winter Session at Seton Hall University. If it was not the first course, it was certainly *one* of the first. The 1-credit course appealed to students for a number of reasons. First, it gave the student a convenient and economical way to obtain that odd credit needed to satisfy a 130-credit requirement for graduation, when most courses were for 3 credits. Also, since it was about baseball, it was a sort of novelty. This course, listed as MATH 1011, is still taught at Seton Hall. Since Winter Session classes are no longer offered at this institution, the course is taught during two Saturdays each spring semester: an 8-hour session in March followed by a 4-hour session in April. The course enjoys a great deal of popularity.

Since in the spring of 1996, MA 488 has been the course number for the 3-credit sabermetrics course which has been offered every year at the United States Military Academy at West Point. As is the case with all 3-credit courses at West Point, forty contact hours are required.

Since we three authors are most familiar with the MATH 1011 and MA 488 courses, this primer reflects our experiences with them. When necessary, because of a divergence of approaches due to the difference in the number of credits, we specify either MATH 1011 or MA 488, as appropriate.

Finally, we have mentioned that other schools also offer sabermetrics courses. Bowling Green State University and Tufts University, for example. We suspect that other schools will be offering similar courses in the near future, believe this because of the many issues which presently surround the national pastime, including economic, ethical, social and cultural concerns.

(B) Prerequisites for Courses on Sabermetrics

For MATH 1011, the prospective student was expected to have a working knowledge of arithmetic, algebra and a bit of descriptive statistics (mean, standard deviation, etc.). A basic four-function calculator, with a square-root key, was also required before the availability of personal laptop computers. In times past, student accessibility to a data source (*Total Baseball*, for example) was also a requirement. Presently, of course, the Internet is used, taking advantage of a plethora of Web sites (see our References section). Students of any major are permitted to take this course, provided he or she obtain approval from an academic advisor.

Regarding the MA 488 course, all students would have passed the four core mathematics courses required of all cadets. These courses include a semester of mathematical modeling, one year of calculus and a semester of probability and statistics. The cadets are also well versed in computer skills and trained to use spreadsheets, such as Excel, and computer algebra systems and statistics packages, like Mathematica and Minitab.

Our experience has taught us that unless a student has a great interest in baseball and a desire to really learn more about the game, it is a mistake for him or her to take a course on sabermetrics. The course is not a trivia course; no student is ever asked to round out the Chicago Cubs infield of Frank Chance, Johnny Evers and Joe Tinker. But, unless there is a passion for the game, and its history — not to mention an appreciation for the essential role of numbers in baseball — the student will soon be bored to tears and wishing to drop the course. Should the student know about Harry Steinfeldt, all the better.

(C) Course Objectives

We start with the Bill James definition of sabermetrics: *the search for objective knowledge about baseball.* This is the *overarching* goal and objective in a course on sabermetrics: to teach the student how to search, measure and assess and draw conclusions.

We strive to teach the student how to reason in a sabermetrical fashion, using as many independent measures and instruments as possible. At the end of the course it is hoped that the student will be able to: 1) frame questions in a well defined manner; 2) if necessary, make reasonable assumptions; 3) use appropriate measures in a critical and proper way; 4) draw reasonable and plausible conclusions; and 5) realize any limitations drawn from the conclusions.

As we have emphasized in this book, to draw sabermetrical conclusions is not the same as proving a mathematical theorem.

(D) Course Content

The following bulleted list refers to MATH 1011. Note that all but the last two bullets refer to the March session; the final two to the April class.

• A diagnostic test to determine the BQ (Baseball Quotient) of the students; this is not graded

- A discussion of the history of baseball, with special emphasis on the development of the statistical measures used in the past
- A short review of algebra and descriptive statistics
- A thorough exposition of the "runs created" school popularized by Bill James
- A thorough exposition of the "linear weights" school, developed by John Thorn and Pete Palmer
- Introduction to other measures such as total average, the total power quotient and the weighted pitcher's rating
- A demonstration of data mining using the Internet
- In-class exercises
- Determination of a course project (must be approved by instructors)
- Topics for open notes examination.
- Course project and briefing
- Final examination

The sequence of the topics above is roughly followed in the MA 488 course as well. However, because that course is weighted for three credits, and because we have many more contact hours, we not only delve more deeply into such topics as data mining, but we explore other topics and use computer technology much more. For example, the cadets might be asked to simulate the following situation: given a batter who hits .400, and has exactly 4 at-bats in each game, how often will he hit safely in 57 or more consecutive games? One can very quickly simulate hundreds of seasons using a random number command in Excel. Furthermore, one can tweak the parameters, such as varying the number of at-bats per game and increasing or decreasing the .400 batting average.

Other topics like clutch play, "streakiness" and ranking great teams of the past are also covered. In-class assignments, projects and examinations are also administered. See Section I below (A Sample of Assessment Instruments) for some examples of these course requirements.

A certain amount of lecturing is unavoidable. Still, we encourage much dialogue, and questions are always welcome, giving the course a seminar flavor. Often we use PowerPoint displays and afterwards have the presentations accessible to the students via the course home page.

Finally, we invite departmental colleagues to address our class if their research interests can be applied to sabermetrics. For example, it can be shown that the distribution of the occurrence of no-hitters can be closely modeled as a Poisson process with a particular exponential distribution studied in statistical analysis, using the assumption that these rare events are memoryless.

(E) In-class Dynamics

In addition to the imparting of knowledge, the opportunity exists to share opinions, perspectives and memories via classroom exchanges. While a course on sabermetrics focuses primarily on the hitting, pitching, running and fielding aspects of major league Baseball, we often have auxiliary discussions which may suggest a project topic for which a particular student may have a special interest. For example, we have had projects submitted concerning the Negro Leagues, women in professional baseball, elections to the Baseball Hall of Fame and the escalation of salaries — all researched from a sabermetrical perspective.

We have instituted many pedagogical changes over the twenty years we have taught sabermetrics courses. The most radical changes have been due to technology. The innumerable Web sites, in addition to split statistics, such as an individual's batting average for day games versus night games, have provided so much data that we often have to filter out extraneous information to address specific questions.

We have found that serious students not only enjoy a course on sabermetrics, but they are generally self-motivated. Once they learn a specific measure which can be applied to an area in which they have an interest, they will often attempt to expand and improve the specific model. In addition, further research may lead them to some very technical sources. For example, in a 1977 article titled "An Offensive Earned-Run Average for Baseball" which appeared in the journal *Operations Research*, authors Thomas Cover and Carroll Keilers use such concepts as "Markov Chains" and "Negative Binomial Distributions" to develop their statistical analysis.

Naturally, as instructors, we strive to present a complete picture of the pertinent material in a simple, clear manner, without compromising the underlying mathematical integrity. We also try to put the development of this material within the rich historical context which major league baseball possesses. Above all, we attempt to provide an atmosphere where we can "talk baseball."

(F) Data Mining and Course Aids

As we have indicated above, the Internet is by far our main source of data. Because most of our students have grown up in this computer age, they are most adept in surfing the Web. Many of them are also skilled in importing data into Excel spreadsheets.

In times past, we used various editions of *Total Baseball* and the

Baseball Encyclopedia to obtain raw statistical totals. *The Hidden Game of Baseball* was, and still is, often referenced, both for its exposition of linear weights and for its insights into the historical development of many of the instruments used in sabermetrics. The same was and is true regarding various *Baseball Abstracts* editions written by Bill James.

Should other hard copy references be required, we encourage our students to use university library book lending programs.

No formal text is required in MATH 1011. We currently use *Curve Ball* in MA 488. Both courses have handouts as supplemental reading.

(G) Outside Speakers and Panels

Over the years we have invited a number of outside speakers to address our classes. For MATH 1011, this has usually taken the form of a panel of baseball fans; individuals who have been following the national pastime since the 1950s. They would share memories about such players as Willie Mays and Mickey Mantle while addressing such questions as whether or not Pete Rose should be inducted into the Hall of Fame. Other questions posed by the students might relate to such topics as free agency, inter-league play and the use of steroids or other banned substances.

We have been privileged to host many guests for our MA 488 sabermetrics class at West Point. Some of these have been:

- Robert Brown, former Yankee third baseman, eminent cardiologist and past President of the American League.
- Steve Balboni, former first baseman with the Yankees, Royals and Mariners, and member of the 1985 World Series champions.
- William Jenkinson, member of SABR, noted expert on long home runs and recent author of *The Year Babe Ruth Hit 104 Home Runs*.

Speakers such as these provide a singular opportunity for the students. How can you sit back and listen to Dr. Bobby Brown without learning something about the game? He played baseball with Joe DiMaggio. Need we say more?

(H) Field Trips

Due to time constraints and the fact that the course is 1-credit, the students who take MATH 1011 do not presently have the opportunity to make field trips.

Over the years during which MA 488 has been offered, students and instructors have made single-day trips to the following facilities:

• The National Baseball Hall of Fame and Museum in Cooperstown, New York
• The Yogi Berra Museum and Learning Center in Montclair, New Jersey
• The offices of *Mlb.com* in New York City
• Yankee Stadium and the administrative offices of the New York Yankees, located in the Bronx.

We had the added pleasure of meeting Yogi Berra during our visit to his museum. Former baseball commissioner Bart Giamatti once remarked that "talking to Yogi Berra about baseball is like speaking to Homer about the gods." Our meeting with Mr. Berra verified Dr. Giamatti's statement.

(I) A Sample of Assessment Instruments: Some Supplemental Problems, Projects, and Examinations

With the exception of the first document below, the assessment instruments have been taken from the MA 488 course. We have not included the solutions to these exercises in case some instructors would want to use these for their classes. Should the reader desire solutions to any of the questions below, please e-mail any of the authors.

MATH 1011 — FINAL EXAMINATION

NAME _____

You are allowed to use your notes for this examination. Calculators are permitted.

1. Barry Bonds's 2001 batting statistics:

G	AB	R	H	2B	3B	HR	RBI	BB
153	476	129	156	32	2	73	137	177

SO	TB	HBP	SF	SH	SB	CS	GIDP
93	411	9	2	0	13	3	5

Use the above data to calculate the following quantities: AVG, OBA, SLG, PRO (OB + SLG), ISO, PwrF, RC (not technical), LWTS, and TPQ.

2. Fibonacci Win Points is a method to determine the value of a pitcher's win-loss record. The formula is: (WINS) × (WPCT) + (WINS OVER .500). For example, Yankee Hall of Famer Whitey Ford had a career record of 236 W, 106 L, for a winning percentage (WPCT) of .690. Therefore, FIB = 236 × .690 + 130 = 293.

Evaluate the five seasons given below by the above criteria. Also, consider their relative ERAs, their pitching linear weights (PLWTS), and compare their winning percentage to that of their teams. Include an analysis of your results. Whose season was the best?

Notes:

• PLWTS= (IP/9) × (ERA-League ERA)
• Relative ERA = League ERA / Individual ERA

Name	W	L	ERA	IP	League ERA	Team's WPCT
Grove, 1931	31	4	2.06	289	4.38	107–45, .704
Dean, 1934	30	7	2.66	312	4.06	95–58, .621
Guidry, 1978	25	3	1.74	274	3.77	100–63, .613
Gooden, 1985	24	4	1.53	276.66	3.59	98–64, .605
Maddux, 1995	19	2	1.63	209.66	4.18	90–54, .625

3. The following is the career offensive record for Mickey Mantle:

	G	AB	R	H	2B	3B	HR	RBI	BB	TB	SB
Mantle	2401	8102	1677	2415	344	72	536	1509	1733	4511	153

Because of injuries, he had less than 10,000 plate appearances (AB + BB). Assuming a 7 percent improvement, find his equivalence coefficient, and use it to project the number of HR he would have had, if his plate appearances had reached 12000.

4. Answer as thoroughly as possible:

There are many in the baseball community who feel that sabermetrics is not a worthwhile study, while others take the opposite approach. In your own words, describe what impact, if any, sabermetrics has had on your understanding of the game. Explain.

MA488
DIAGNOSTIC TEST

1. Name a team that played in the first World Series.

2. What year was the first World Series?

3. Who stroked 257 hits in 1920, setting the seasonal record which lasted over eighty years?

4. Who broke the seasonal hit record set in 1920 and how many hits did he amass?

5. What is the formula for slugging percentage?

Match the players to their nicknames:

6. Babe Ruth_____   A. The Big Hurt

7. Pete Rose_____   B. The Big Unit

8. Joe DiMaggio_____   C. The Big Train

9. Davy Force_____   D. Big Mac

10. Randy Johnson_____   E. The Bambino

11. Mark McGwire_____   F. Tom Thumb

12. Grover Alexander_____   G. The Splendid Splinter

13. Frank Thomas_____   H. Charlie Hustle

14. Ted Williams_____   I. Old Pete

15. Walter Johnson_____   J. The Yankee Clipper

K. The Georgia Peach

L. Mr. October

16. Who was the oldest rookie to play in the Major Leagues: Minnie Minoso, Jackie Robinson or Satchel Paige?

17. How many current MLB teams have never won a World Series?

18. Who holds the record for the highest lifetime batting average?

19. How many different ways can a batter reach first base?

20. What is your favorite major league team?

KEY: 16–20 correct, All-Star; 11–15 correct, Free Agent; 0–10 correct, Rookie

MA488
PROJECT: PROJECTION

Bo Jackson wasn't the first multisport athlete, but he was one of the best. His feats in both major league baseball and the National Football League are well-known, and the outfielder/running back became the first athlete named to two sports' All-Star games, a testament to his athletic prowess. After winning the Heisman Trophy and TSN College Football Player of the Year in 1985, Jackson opted to sign with the Kansas City Royals instead of the NFL's Tampa Bay Buccaneers. He joined the Royals after just 53 games in the minors and, while showing speed and power, he struck out frequently and displayed questionable defense.

After showing improvement in 1987 with 22 HR despite 158 strike-outs, Bo announced his plan to play football in the off-season with the Raiders as "a hobby," a move initially not appreciated by Kansas City players or fans. In 1988 Jackson slammed 25 homers and stole 27 bases but still struck out 146 times. However, in 1989 he finally raised his batting average, to .256, hit 32 HR with 105 RBI, and used his speed and strong arm to become one of the most exciting left fielders in baseball. That same year, Jackson was named to the AL All-Star team, and proceeded to win the MVP Award of the game, after bashing a titanic home run off the Giants' Rick Reuschel. When the baseball season ended, Jackson returned to the Raiders in full force, and was named to the Pro Bowl just five months after playing the Major League Baseball All-Star game. Bo's lifetime totals for the following categories are as follows:

AB	2393
BB	200
H	598
2B	86
3B	14
HR	141
R	341
RBI	415
HBP	14

Using the concept of Equivalence Coefficient (EC), extend Jackson's total plate appearances to 8,000. Assume that he would decline in performance at a rate of 2.5 percent (as football took a toll on his body). Determine the following:

AB	H	TB	HR	RBI	BA	SLG	ISO	PwrF	PA	RC

Prior to the recent power explosion, 500 career home runs was almost a guarantee for that player to get into the Baseball Hall of Fame. What EC would Bo Jackson have to maintain to project his home run total to that milestone?

References

Baseball-Reference.com. http://www.baseball-reference.com/
"Bo Jackson." BaseballLibrary.com. http://www.baseballlibrary.com/baseball library/ballplayers/J/Jackson_Bo.stm.
Retrosheet. http://www.retrosheet.org.

MA488
PROJECT: MODELING A "GOOD" PITCHER

What are the traits of a good pitcher? Control, durability, determination, power, the ability to induce a double play, or the ability to get a strikeout.

The Baseball Archive (http://www.baseball1.com/statistics) provides pitching data for over 100 years.

1. Use the data for 2004 to develop a model that predicts the number of wins per games started. You must decide which data to include. Consider normalizing your data; for example, use hits per inning.

2. Use the data for 2004 to develop a model that predicts the effectiveness of closers.

3. Compare your models to models that you develop in two other eras.

4. Use these models to discuss how pitching has changed.

5. Use your models to select a staff of 5 starters and 2 closers using the 2006 data.

MA488
PROJECT: MODELING BINARY OUTCOMES IN BASEBALL

1. Identify a Binary Baseball Outcome you would like to examine and predict. Examples (think of others):

   • Wins/Losses in games — predict using either a player's stats (as in class example) or team stats (errors in the game, hits in the game, HRs in the game etc.)
   • Team makes the playoffs or doesn't — could use any number of predictors: ERA, fielding pct. (pitching and defense win championships), batting average, etc.
   • Player makes Hall of Fame or not

2. Collect data to try to build a model for predicting the outcome (note: start early and let instructors know if you have problems finding the data).

3. Using logistic regression, build a model (or models) to predict the response. Clearly describe the predictors you tried, and how you decided on your final model.

4. For the final model, check goodness of fit as well as model assumptions. Are there any influential observations in the data? If so, why (and how do they impact the model)?

5. Regardless of whether your model is significant or not, interpret the results. What are the model-based probabilities of your outcome for various values of the predictors? What are the odds ratios for the predictors, and what do they tell you?

6. What conclusions can you draw about predicting your outcome? What, if anything, might allow you to improve your model is you had more time or data?

MA 488
IN-CLASS ASSIGNMENT: THE DESIGNATED HITTER

Ten Arguments For

1. Since 1973 it has "modernized" baseball.

2. Baseball must change with the times.

3. Virtually every league (except the NL) uses it.

4. Real baseball fans want offense.

5. Pitchers can't hit.

6. Older, great hitters can still hit.

7. There is no advantage for the AL/NL regarding inter-league play.

8. "Specialists" are good for baseball.

9. There is more strategy with the DH.

10. (Write your own.)

Ten Arguments Against

1. Since 1973, "pure" baseball doesn't exist.

2. Baseball should retain its tradition.

3. It should be banned in every other league.

4. Real baseball fans want pitching and defense.

5. Pitchers can hit.

6. Older, great hitters can't run or field.

7. The AL/NL has an advantage over the NL/AL regarding inter-league play.

8. "Specialists" are bad for baseball.

9. There is more strategy without the DH.

10. (Write your own.)

A Question Regarding the Boston Red Sox (c. 1914)

You are "Rough" Carrigan, the manager of the Red Sox. There's this left-handed pitcher from Baltimore. He's got a lot to learn, but an awful lot of potential. Do you spend every bit of time with him polishing up his pitching skills, or do you waste his time and yours letting him hit in batting practice?

MA488
IN-CLASS ASSIGNMENT: A WEIGHTED
FIBONACCI APPROACH TO PREDICTION

Introduction: Bill James has used a "Fibonacci Approach" in some of his research. One basic application of this idea is to go back two seasons to "predict" a statistic for an upcoming season. Let us consider a modification to this, in an attempt to derive a statistic which will predict the number of home runs a player will hit as he approaches the prime of his career.

Example: Babe Ruth hit 467 HRs in the 1920s; this is still the record for any decade. In 1925 he was 30 years old. Suppose we try to anticipate his home run total for 1925, based on his two previous seasons.

- In 1923, Ruth hit 41 HR in 522 AB for a home run ratio (HRR) of 0.0785
- In 1924, Ruth hit 46 HR in 529 AB for a HRR of 0.0870

Let us define Ruth's 1925 Weighted Fibonacci HRR (WFHRR) as

$$WFHRR_{1925} = (1/3)HRR_{1923} + (2/3)HRR_{1924} = (1/3)(0.0785) + (2/3)(0.0870) = 0.0842.$$

Assuming Ruth would have 525 AB in 1925, his predicted HR total would be 44.

Follow Up: Ruth actually hit 25 HR in 1925. He was only 30 years old. What happened?

Questions: Is this a reasonable predictor? If so, over what time interval? Should the "weights" be changed? How many yearly AB should be assumed?

Class Exercise: Using the above definition, predict the following seasonal HR totals for the following sluggers:

• Hack Wilson	1930		• Willie Mays	1965
• Jimmie Foxx	1932		• George Foster	1977
• Hank Greenberg	1938		• Mark McGwire	1998
• Willie Mays	1955		• Sammy Sosa	1998
• Roger Maris	1961		• Barry Bonds	2003

Now, use a scatter plot to compare their predicted HR totals with the actual total. Is this a good predictor?

MA 488
IN-CLASS ASSIGNMENT: TIME TRAVEL

Scenario: The year is 2040. You are enjoying your partnership with a fellow USMA graduate, getting richer by the hour. Your expertise involves financial consultation, while limiting your clients to MLB players, past and present.

You travel to the year 2008 in your new 2040 Chronosphere. Your firm has been tasked to determine:

- The seasonal total power quotient (TPQ) for your each of your clients

- The seasonal *relative* TPQ for each of your clients: $\dfrac{TPQ_{Individual}}{TPQ_{Major\ Leagues}}$

Once these figures are determined, you will renegotiate the contacts of your clients, based on your research.

$$TPQ = \frac{HR + TB + RBI}{AB}$$

Economic Consultation Firm	*Clients*	*Year*
Black & Red Associates of Western Pennsylvania	Ty Cobb	1911
	Gavvy Cravath	1915
	Babe Ruth	1920
	Babe Ruth	1921
	George Sisler	1922
	Lou Gehrig	1927
Blue & White Finances of California	Hack Wilson	1930
	Jimmie Foxx	1932
	Joe DiMaggio	1937
	Hank Greenberg	1938
	Ted Williams	1941
	Mickey Mantle	1956
Brown & Green Planning of New England	Ted Williams	1957
	Roger Maris	1961
	Willie Mays	1965
	Mark McGwire	1998
	Barry Bonds	2001
	Barry Bonds	2002

MA 488 Midterm Examination

READ THESE INSTRUCTIONS CAREFULLY BEFORE STARTING WORK.

1. Place all textbooks, etc., neatly in the hallway.
2. Print your name and section on every sheet used.
3. For this examination, references authorized are:
   a. Notes
   b. Calculator
   c. Laptop computer (no wireless/Internet access)
4. Sufficient work is required to indicate clearly the method of reasoning and the operations performed. SHOW ALL WORK. Clearly indicate your final answer.
5. All work written on the WPR will be graded unless marked through or explicitly marked with words to the effect of "do not grade."
6. Work only on the front side of a sheet of paper. If you need more space, use a separate sheet for each problem continued. Clearly indicate which problem is continued by writing "*Cont'd on sheet* ____" on the problem sheet and "*Prob* ____ *cont'd*" on the additional sheet. Be sure to put your name on the continuation sheet.
7. Early departure is authorized. Place completed WPRs in the instructor folder on the instructor's desk.

Question 1

Henry Benjamin Greenberg's career spanned from 1930 through 1947, playing all but one year for the Detroit Tigers. A right-handed slugging first baseman, his power rivaled that of Lou Gehrig and Jimmie Foxx. Greenberg was among the first major league players to enter into military service during World War II, which caused him to lose approximately four years of active play. Nevertheless, Greenberg amassed 331 home runs (HR) in 5193 at-bats (AB). He also walked (W) 844 times.

   a) Project Hank Greenberg's home run total if he had a total of 13,000 plate appearances (AB + W), and assuming he would have been 3 percent better (the "kicker") during the years he missed.
   b) Given the same number of additional AB and W as above, what "kicker" would be needed to give a projected HR total of 713?
   c) Consider Greenberg's original totals. Find the number of additional AB needed to arrive at a HR total of 713 if he was 3 percent better during these additional AB.
   d) Do these results seem reasonable?

Question 2

An "All Subsets" regression in MINITAB based on pitching statistics from 1876–1881 yields the following output.

Response is w/gs

Vars	R-Sq	R-Sq(adj)	Mallows C-p	S	BAOpp	ERA	so/lbb	whip	IP/GS	SHO
1	33.2	32.4	6.4	0.16629	X					
1	29.6	28.9	11.4	0.17062				X		
2	37.0	35.6	3.0	0.16236	X					X
2	34.3	32.9	6.8	0.16575	X				X	
3	38.5	36.4	3.0	0.16137	X				X	X
3	37.8	35.6	4.0	0.16231	X	X				X
4	39.4	36.6	3.6	0.16104	X	X			X	X
4	39.1	36.3	4.1	0.16146	X			X	X	X
5	39.6	36.1	5.4	0.16172	X		X	X	X	X
5	39.5	35.9	5.5	0.16190	X	X	X		X	X
6	39.9	35.6	7.0	0.16233	X	X	X	X	X	X

a. Suggest which variable(s) to incorporate in an appropriate model to predict wins per game started. Clearly explain what criterion guided your choice.

b. List one of the guiding assumptions in multiple regression and describe how you would go about checking its validity.

Question 3

You are a New York sportswriter preparing an article comparing the Hall-of-Fame credentials of Gil Hodges and Don Mattingly. Discuss how you would use MINITAB to make an informed comparison.

Question 4

Starting pitchers are asked to pitch more innings in each game than relief pitchers (even in today's game of specialists). As a result, a batter usually has more than one chance to "see" the pitcher — arguably an advantage for the hitter in later at bats. Thus, one might expect that each time through the batting order a pitcher is likely to get hit more heavily. The data in the Minitab project "fy072 wpr time through order data.MPJ" consists of a random sample of 30 pitchers with at least 25 innings pitched to hitter a faced a third time in a game. The data itself includes the name of the pitcher (Player), the pitcher's team (Team), then the number of games (G), innings pitched (IP) and earned run average (ERA) for each pitcher for a given time seeing the batter in the ballgame. The final variable (Order) gives which time through the order the pitcher statistics refer to, with a 1 meaning the 1st time through the order and thus facing a batter, 2 the 2nd time though, 3 the 3rd time and 4 meaning 4th (or more) time through the order. Use this data to answer the questions below.

a) Ignoring the player, is there a statistical difference in pitcher ERA based upon which time through the batting order? (Support your answer.)

b) Does accounting for the player in the model change the results? (Support your answer.) Does this answer surprise you? (Explain why or why not.)

c) Using either model from a) or b), which (if any) times through the order differ statistically and how? (If none differ, which are closest to having a statistical difference?)

d) Examine the model assumptions for the model you chose in c) Is there anything of concern? (Explain.)

e) What is one possible problem with answering this question using the data provided? (Explain.)

MA 488 Term-end Examination

READ THESE INSTRUCTIONS CAREFULLY BEFORE STARTING WORK.

1. Place all textbooks, etc., neatly in the hallway.
2. Print your name and section on every sheet used.
3. For this examination, references authorized are:
   a. Notes
   b. Calculator
   c. Laptop computer (no wireless/Internet access)

4. Sufficient work is required to indicate clearly the method of reasoning and the operations performed. SHOW ALL WORK. Clearly indicate your final answer.

5. All work written on the WPR will be graded unless marked through or explicitly marked with words to the effect of "do not grade."

6. Work only on the front side of a sheet of paper. If you need more space, use a separate sheet for each problem continued. Clearly indicate which problem is continued by writing "*Cont'd on sheet* _____" on the problem sheet and "*Prob* _____ *cont'd*" on the additional sheet. Be sure to put your name on the continuation sheet.

7. Early departure is authorized. Place completed WPRs in the instructor folder on the instructor's desk.

Question 1

Use sabermetrical arguments to determine the best season enjoyed by the following six Hall-of-Fame center fielders:

Ty Cobb	1911
Tris Speaker	1916
Joe DiMaggio	1937
Duke Snider	1955
Mickey Mantle	1957
Willie Mays	1965

Question 2

Discuss the both the validity and the shortcomings of the concept of the *equivalence coefficient*. Modify the instrument so as to make it a more realistic model for prediction.

Question 3

Consider the following five pitchers enshrined in the Hall of Fame:

Steve Carlton	Nolan Ryan
Whitey Ford	Tom Seaver
Sandy Koufax	

Determine the pitcher with the highest proficiency (P) using the following model:

$$P = \sqrt{W} + \left(\frac{K}{100} \right) + \left(\frac{90}{ERA} \right) - \sqrt[3]{L}$$

Question 4

Compare the records of Barry Bonds and Frank Thomas over the years 1990–1995.

Question 5

Discuss sabermetrics. Has it really changed how professional baseball is viewed and assessed? Include both qualitative and quantitative components, as well as personal opinions, in your discussion.

MA 488
HALL OF FAME IDENTIFICATIONS

1. I was known as "The Flying Dutchman" and was a member of the first class, elected in 1936.
2. I was the third baseman in Connie Mack's famed "$100,000 Infield" of the early 1900s, and I had a very powerful nickname.
3. I am actually in the Football Hall of Fame. Babe Ruth replaced me as an outfielder when he came to the Yankees.
4. I am also in the Football Hall of Fame (as a player) and in the Baseball Hall of Fame as an umpire.
5. Yankee backstop Bill Dickey "learned me" how to catch.
6. During the latter years of my life, I was known as "Baseball's Greatest Living Player," but I was not immediately elected to the Hall of Fame when I retired.
7. I hit the first World Series home run in Yankee Stadium, but I'm mostly remembered as a manager.
8. Our first names are Robert, Vernon and Steve, but we were all known as "Lefty."

9. I was known as "The Mechanical Man" and played second base for some great Tiger teams.

10. In 1910, New York columnist Franklin P. Adams wrote a famous poem which immortalized the three of us.

11. I was known as "The Grey Eagle" when I roamed center field during the first quarter of the 20th century.

12. I have the highest percentage of votes ever garnered for an elected member of the Hall of Fame.

13. We played in different eras, but both of us suffered tragic and premature deaths, so any waiting periods before our elections were waived.

14. I was known as "Little Napoleon."

15. I was honored to be called the "Grand Old Man of Baseball."

16. I was the last of the "legitimate" spitball pitchers and was known as "Old Stubblebeard."

17. I hit a line drive which broke Dizzy Dean's toe in the 1937 All-Star Game.

18. Ty Cobb helped me with my hitting; so much so, that I won four American League batting titles in alternate years in the 1920s.

(J) Student Feedback

Over the years, we have had very few complaints about our courses on sabermetrics. Many times, especially with the MATH 1011 course, students ask about the possibility of a "Sabermetrics II" course or the feasibility of offering the course for three credits. All students complete end-of-course surveys which attempt to assess the learning of the student in the course. How was the mix of mathematics with "baseball pedagogy"? Did the projects and exams sufficiently test their knowledge? As mentioned above, some students have submitted papers or given presentations at regional mathematics meetings, based on their sabermetrics projects. Feedback is always requested, and we have been pleased with the results.

Baseball is still popular. Despite the surrounding controversies, the national pastime is still that. It would be difficult to conceive of many things which would be more enjoyable than teaching people about baseball.

References: An Informal Bibliography and Websites

Books

Albert, Jim, and Jay Bennett. *Curve Ball: Baseball, Statistics, and the Role of Chance in the Game* (Rev. Ed.). New York: Copernicus Books, 2003.

Hoban, Michael. *Baseball's Complete Players: Ratings of Total-Season Performance for the Greatest Players of the 20th Century.* Jefferson, N.C.: McFarland, 2000.

James, Bill. *The Bill James Baseball Abstract.* (Various editions) New York: Ballantine Books.

_____. *The Bill James Historical Baseball Abstract.* (Various editions) New York: Villard Books.

_____, John Dewan, Neil Munro, and Don Zminda, eds. *STATS™ ALL-TIME baseball Sourcebook.* Skokie, IL: STATS, Inc, 1998.

_____, and Jim Henzler. *Win Shares.* Morton Grove, IL: STATS, Inc., 2002.

Jenkinson, Bill. *The Year Babe Ruth hit 104 Home Runs.* New York: Carroll and Graf Publishers, 2007.

Schwartz, Alan. *The Numbers Game.* New York: St. Martin's Press, 2004.

Thorn, John, and Pete Palmer. *The Hidden Game of Baseball.* New York: Doubleday, 1985.

Thorn, John, and Pete Palmer, eds. *Total Baseball.* 2nd ed. New York: Warner Books, 1991.

Williams, Ted, and Jim Prime. *Ted Williams' Hit List.* Indianapolis: Masters, 1996.

Articles

Albert, J. "Exploring baseball hitting data: what about those breakdown statistics?" *Journal of the American Statistical Association* 89 (1994), pp. 1066–1074.

Lindsey, G. "An Investigation of Strategies in Baseball." *Operations Research* (1963), pp. 120–127.

Smith, D. "Maury Wills and the Value of a Stolen Base." *Baseball Research Journal* (1980).

Web Sites

Baseball Almanac. http://www.baseball-almanac.com.

Baseball Prospectus. Prospectus Entertainment Ventures. http://www.baseballpro
spectus.com/.

Baseball-Reference.com: Major League Baseball Statistics and History Sports Reference, Inc. http://www.baseball-reference.com.

Baseball Think Factory. http://www.baseballthinkfactory.org.

"Consecutive Games Hitting Streaks." http://www.baseball-almanac.com/feats/feats-
streak.shtml.

Hello Baseball Fans! http://www.hellobaseballfans.com.

High Boskage House Baseball-Analysis Web Site. http://www.highboskage.com.

Mike Emeigh's Baseball Page. http://www.geocities.com/Colosseum/Stadium/8957.

"*Official Rules.*" Major League Baseball. http://mlb.mlb.com/mlb/official_info/
official_rules/foreword.jsp.

Paul Wendt homepage. http://world.std.com/~pgw.

POP™ AWARD. Perfect Players Partners Ltd. http://www.popaward.com/htdocs/
Index.htm.

Retrosheet. http://www.retrosheet.org.

Rob Neyer column. ESPN.com. http://espn.go.com/mlb/columns/neyer_rob.

Rob Neyer homepage. http://www.robneyer.com.

"Science of Baseball." Exploratorium.
http://www.Exploratorium.edu/baseball.

Sinins Lee. "Around the Majors." *The Hardball Times.* http://www.hardballtimes.
com/main/atm.

Tango on Baseball. Tom N. Tango. http://www.tangotiger.net.

Index

About the Authors

Gabriel B. Costa is a Roman Catholic priest, ordained for service in 1979 for the Archdiocese of Newark, New Jersey. He is also a mathematician and is on an extended academic leave from Seton Hall University. He is a professor of mathematical sciences at the United States Military Academy, located at West Point, New York, where he also functions as an associate chaplain. He is a member of SABR and has published in *The Baseball Research Journal, Elysian Fields Quarterly* and other journals. He has been a Yankees fan since he was 10 years old in 1958.

Michael Huber is an associate professor of mathematics at Muhlenberg College. He was a co-teacher of sabermetrics at the United States Military Academy with Father Gabriel Costa from 1996 to 2006. His book, *West Point's Field of Dreams: Major League Baseball at Doubleday Field*, was published in 2004 by Vermont Heritage Press, chronicling 87 exhibition games played between Army cadets and major league baseball teams. A lifelong baseball fan, he enjoys rooting for the Baltimore Orioles, attending minor league games, and modeling rare events in baseball, such as triple plays, no-hitters, and hitting for the cycle.

John T. Saccoman is an associate professor of mathematics and computer science at Seton Hall University in New Jersey. He team-teaches one of the earliest known sabermetrics courses there with its founder, Father Gabriel Costa. His work has appeared in numerous SABR publications, including *Deadball Stars of the National League, Deadball Stars of the American League,* and *The Fenway Project*. He has contributed biographies of Gil Hodges and Willie Mays, among others, to the SABR Bio Project. A charter member of the Elysian Fields (NJ) Chapter of SABR, John resides in northern New Jersey with his son (and fellow Mets fan) Ryan and Bosox-loving wife Mary.